P9-DEW-719

Garage

Garage

Reinventing the Place We Park

KIRA OBOLENSKY

The Taunton Press

The Taunton Press
Inspiration for hands-on living™

The Taunton Press, Inc., 63 South Main Street, PO Box 5506, Newtown, CT 06470-5506
e-mail: tp@taunton.com

Distributed by Publishers Group West

DESIGN AND LAYOUT: Susan Fazekas

ILLUSTRATOR: Scott Bricher

LIBRARY OF CONGRESS CATALOGING-IN-PUBLICATION DATA:
Obolensky, Kira.
    Garage : reinventing the place we park / Kira Obolensky.
        p. cm.
    ISBN 1-56158-378-2
    1. Garages–United States. I. Title.
NA8348 .O26 2001
728'.98–dc21   2001027685

Printed in Singapore
10 9 8 7 6 5 4 3 2 1

For Irve,

who needs a bigger garage.

Acknowledgments

This book started and ended with a question, which I asked hundreds of times, at cocktail parties, at neighborhood gatherings, of friends and acquaintances. The question "Know of any interesting garages?" is not only a good ice breaker, it always gets answered. I want to thank every person who answered that question for me. Even if the response didn't make it into this book (I'm thinking of a garage covered entirely with squirrel tails), I am grateful for the chance to have contemplated such a vision.

A short list of people who contributed with interest, knowledge, and garage tips includes: Lynn Barnhouse, Tom Oliphant, Julie Briskman, Lynn Wadsworth, Betsy Williams, Laurie Liss, Linda Mack, Dick Kronick, Michael Koop, Jim Walsh, and Tara Devereux. Paul Buum acted as technical consultant. Thanks to Mary Ludington for her good photos and company. Thanks also to Leslie Goat, who wrote a stunning dissertation on the history of the American garage, and who really is a garage expert.

The people who worked on this book at The Taunton Press deserve kudos, particularly given some of the strange twists and turns we took together: Carol Kasper, Steve Culpepper, and Peter Chapman were all wonderful to work with. Thanks also to Wendi Mijal for helping with photographs and to Paula Schlosser for her design sense.

And my thanks go to everyone who opened their garage doors to me.

Contents

Introduction

The idea that you can do something other than park your car in the garage was already prevalent when I was growing up in the 1960s and '70s in suburban Houston. When I was a kid, I played in my neighbor's garage, and I went to church in a different garage. Nondescript on the outside, the latter garage was attached to a rambler out near the airport and was a temporary solution to a building project that was going to bring a Russian Orthodox church to the area. There was something downright surreal about driving up, hitting a garage-door opener, and seeing the door rise on a world of incense, icons, and older Russian ladies (mostly astrophysicists in the Old Country). The garage, while not the epicenter of my childhood social life, certainly captured the overflow.

Maybe it's that childhood vision of the garage door opening onto another, more extraordinary world that gives me such a sense of the possibilities that lurk behind garage doors. Without a doubt, the weirdest garage I ever saw had dust from every country in the Western world and eggs in it shaped like question marks. Such a collection was amassed by a Midwestern milkman, whose creative passion found its rightful place in his backyard alley. The most beautiful garage? Mindful that garage beauty is a subjective thing, I'd suggest that there's a garage in Wisconsin that

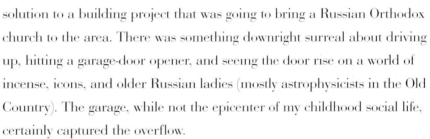

The athlete's garage: **This garage has barnlike proportions and a built-in basketball court.**

This California garage is big enough for an MG and a metal shop.

The ubiquitous garage basketball hoop— with plenty of driveway— turns any garage into a neighborhood court.

shimmers like a castle on the hill. The most poetic garage: a solitary space with a screen door and a simple cot for naps. The messiest garage was in Texas and its owner a collector of used automobile parts and geodes, mattresses, and pocketknives, all of which found their home in a series of garagelike sheds.

While the attic holds memories of the past, the garage lives in the present tense. If the house is the ego, the garage is the id of the domestic setting. It's a container—for cars, certainly, but also for the dreams and passions of the house's occupant.

My own garage was built for a Model T, and then someone later added a little extension out the front. Right now, my garage is nothing more than a container with potential: In a snowstorm it holds the Volvo, and the rest of the time it houses the things we like to use when it's warm, like bicycles and gardening equipment.

From the moment we moved into this house, we've considered the garage as a place of great potential. At any point in time, it can serve to answer—at least, conceptually—the latest problem our 1918 Prairie School home presents. At one time we considered turning the garage into a guest

In the *Garage*

Proving the adaptable nature of the garage, this modest structure has been transformed into a backyard screened porch. The sitting area is where the car parking stall used to be.

THIS BOOK IS ABOUT GARAGES. It's about time garages got their own book. Porches, another uniquely American entity, are written about endlessly. That's probably because the porch, which is really useful only for dozing or for watching the neighbors, is considered romantic.

The garage, on the other hand, is not only viable as a place for romance it's also the most adaptable place on the American streetscape. The garage can earn its keep as a workshop, office, greenhouse, art studio, and a place to park the car. You can even turn a garage into a porch.

Square foot for square foot, no other structure has quite the same versatility. Offering advantages such as no commute and low rent, the garage has become a haven and workshop of choice for many people with new ideas. Some of this century's most extraordinary ventures began in someone's garage. Walt

Like a Chinese paper lantern, this modern garage glows in the night. The walls are paneled with translucent corrugated fiberglass, which is durable and relatively inexpensive.

It's not clear which of his hit songs he's playing, but you know he's got the crowd rocking with him: Buddy Holly, yet another product of the all-purpose home garage.

Disney, the Hewlett-Packard guys, Amazon.com, and bands like Nirvana and Buddy Holly and the Crickets all got their start in the humble garage. It's probably safe to say that without the garage, we would be still living in the Dark Ages. Or if not the Dark Ages, we'd at least inhabit a world that's less rich in cartoons, rock and roll, and high-tech innovation.

The guy down the street from me does woodworking in his garage on warmer weekends. "Why the garage?" I ask. "Because the basement's too hard to get to," he says. And then there's the gardener who starts her annuals in a garage greenhouse; the teenage drummer who practices in the garage; an inventor who tinkers beneath the buzz of a garage's fluorescent lights. Whether you dream of a victory garden or a mega-computer business, the place to do it is just down the drive-

It's probably safe to say that without the garage, we would be still living in the Dark Ages.

This is an ordinary structure that's used in an extraordinary way—further visual proof that even the most basic of garages can be useful for storage.

People who love vehicles tend to build temples for them. With spotless floors and dramatic lighting, this garage in Massachusetts is a museum for motorcycles.

way. Garages, with their rough-and-ready interiors, can accommodate hobbies as well as grand visions.

Because America is filled with people who invent and dream and plan and collect, there are lots of interesting garages. There are even some garages that, by all accounts, are famous because someone did something so interesting there it became catalogued in the American way of life (see p. 17 for some examples). Famous or not, the garages featured in this book are used for those things in modern life that don't fit in the house. They are humble, sometimes messy, glamorous, funky, but always eminently practical.

With seasonal regularity, this garage holds cars in the winter and functions as a potting shed during the summer months.

Be it ever so humble, **there's no place like the garage.**

A Brief History of the American Garage

According to garage legend, the man who invented the first car also came up with the first place to put it. Henry Ford was born when Lincoln was president and trains were the fastest machines on wheels. He went on to become the father of the Ford Motor Co. and the man who brought the assembly line to car production—both of which would transform the automobile from a plaything of the wealthy to an everyday necessity.

In 1896, Ford was working in a neighbor's coal shed near his home in Detroit, trying to invent an engine that could power a chassis. His tinkering resulted in the first "horseless carriage" (which he called a Quadricycle), a buggy frame on four bicycle wheels powered by a 4-hp engine. That was the car. The garage came about when

This former coal shed **is the equivalent of the Garden of Eden—the place where the car and garage as we know them supposedly all began. Henry Ford is said to have designed the first car here and, after busting down a wall to get it out, the first place to keep it.**

Ford discovered that the vehicle was too big for the coal shed's door. So he busted open a brick wall, making what might be considered the very first garage door. At least that's the story.

From "car house" to "garage"

Garage history begins when the car rolled onto the scene. Carriage houses and stables were similar to the garage: They were also designed to shelter some method of transportation. So the first inclina-

Henry Ford's garage workshop near Detroit was a neighbor's coal shed. He went there to tinker, and his experimentation led to the Quadricycle, the first "horseless carriage," which rolled on bicycle wheels.

Early garages, like this one built in 1900 for the New York industrialist Henry Frick, were designed to hold several cars as well as adequate living quarters for a full-time chauffeur.

Many early garages were combination affairs, built for both horses and cars.

An early three-car garage in Upstate New York obviously belonged to a person of means. Notice the unique motoring ornamentation—garage-door windows in the shape of steering wheels.

tion was to try and put the car into the carriage house or the stable, both of which proved to be a miserable fit. In 1902, a British magazine called *The Car* published a letter from an enterprising doctor suggesting a solution: "I've been able to let the stables and I've put up a Car House in the garden. When the motor is not in use, it can rest in its house for an indefinite period without being any the worse."

In America we preferred the word "garage." The word was elegant (certainly more so than "Car House"), and it was French, from *garer*—to shelter. It rolled off the tongue with the same élan as other French words that entered the vocabulary (*à la carte, rêverie, touché*). The wealthy, who bought the first cars, built the first garages. They were also the same people who had built grand carriage houses and stables, reflecting the prevalent upper-crust notion that the horse should be treated like a gentleman. Apparently, they felt the same way about the automobile. Henry Frick, the American industrialist, owned

several houses and garages. His garage in upstate New York shows his predilection for collecting cars.

Designed to hold a small fleet of cars, as well as workshop space and living space for the chauffeur, these early garages even included built-in car washes, and gas and kerosene pumps. A garage designed for Mr. Dane, which was published in a 1906 issue of *House and Garden*, had room for cars, a workshop, and wash area, as well as a squash court—all on just the first floor.

The multitask garage

Garages that did something other than hold automobiles were considered practical by early garage builders. So why on earth would a combination garage/aviary or a garage that doubled as clock tower be a practical investment? Because the car was still new, and some people didn't want to invest in a structure just for the car. If the car were suddenly replaced with something even more revolutionary or the industrialized world decided that the horse was, after all, simply a better idea, then these forward-thinking folks wouldn't have a useless structure sitting in their driveway.

Many early garages were combination affairs, built for both horses and cars. As a writer of the time pointed out, "When a garage is combined with a stable, it is necessary to keep the former entirely separate from the latter. Otherwise ammonia coming from the stable will tarnish the metal workings of the cars." (The writer neglects to mention the effect the car and its gasoline had on the workings of the horse.)

The democratic garage

When the car became affordable to the middle class, the garage began to lose its mystique. By 1917, there were 458,000 cars on the road. Suddenly, there came a pressing need for a place to keep them. For car owners in big cities, multicar parking garages were the best option. For those who didn't have access to parking garages and lived in

Built in California, this garage holds the car and also manages to tell the time: It's a clock tower.

The garage was removed from the house because of fears about gasoline and fires.

houses without an existing stable or carriage house, there were usually two options: portable garages and prefabricated garages.

An advertisement of the time described the portable garage as "erected by any help of ordinary intelligence and quickly taken down and transported to any place you may care to go." These nifty garages were a do-it-yourself solution to a pressing problem and were designed to be literally portable. The idea was that if you were driving a long distance, you might arrive, garageless, in a place where you would need to park. Hodgson Portable Homes offered a portable garage for $140.

Catalogs like Sears Roebuck sold prefabricated garage kits until the 1940s. A barrel-shaped version is shown in the photo below. These garages were built to contain the car, and they were almost always erected on the service alley, which appeared earlier in the previous century for expedient, discreet deliveries and trash collection. The garage was removed from the house because of fears about gasoline and fires. It was a reasonable concern: Before the advent of the gas station, most automobile owners bought gas in bulk, storing it in the garage along with the car.

A barrel-shaped portable garage, shown in a 1916 edition of *Sunset* magazine, was built by a man from Spokane, Washington, who claimed that the garage could be dismantled in 15 minutes using only a wrench.

The integrated garage

So why did the garage leave its position in the back of the house? Convenience. Once the fear of fire had subsided, thanks in part to concrete and other fire-resistant building materials, it didn't take long for Americans to figure out that schlepping down the driveway with a bag of groceries was not nearly as convenient as popping out of the car directly into the kitchen.

There was a small campaign, waged in housing publications of the 1930s and '40s, to bring the garage closer to the house. "The Garage's Place Is in the Home," intoned a Mr. Burton Ashford Bugbee in a 1932 issue of *House Beautiful*. Mr. Bugbee described status-quo garages as "distressing rows of auto kennels" and passionately cried for "integration"—his term for bringing the garage in from the backyard.

By the 1940s, new garages were built primarily on the side of the house, with a door that opened directly into the kitchen. As Howard Leland Smith counseled from his position as chief architect of the Federal Housing Administration, an attached garage worked better and made the house look bigger. Smith suggested that builders avoid placing garage doors in any position other than at the front of the house. Such advice inspired a garage that was utilitarian in nature and designed for parking and some storage. Sometimes, the garage continued the architecture of the house, but usually its design was not so carefully considered. These garages signaled the beginning of decades of boring garages, which in turn affected the look of the American streetscape.

As for garage function, the overflow from the house came to the garage in the 1950s, when books like *Popular Mechanics' How To Build a Garage* offered suggestions on creating garages that could serve various functions, such as defense against atomic attack. Here's an example:

"Although your home might not have a basement where the family could go to a special shored-up corner for protection in the event of an

This suburban streetscape, **circa 1950s, appears to be half town houses and half garage doors.**

Owned by the movie star **Dennis Hopper,** this garage is the epitome of cool California elegance. With a glass-block floor and corrugated-steel walls, this garage is as spare and clean as a gallery. In fact, it displays both cars and a collection of contemporary art.

atomic attack, you can still provide them with the security and protection of a concrete shelter, without digging a huge hole in your backyard, by incorporating one right in your new garage."

While there are fewer garage atomic shelters built today, the garage has become the one place in the domestic environment that can be anything. It can also be designed and built with other functions than parking in mind. And when the cars add to the architecture of the house—Elvis Presley considered that his fleet of Cadillacs improved the front of Graceland—then the garage can be the first front in home renovation.

Some Notable Garages

We've made it our collective business to identify rooms with the people who've slept in them, houses with the people who lived in them, and cities with the people born in them. And like towns such as Sauk Center, Minnesota, and Wilmington, Delaware, the place is often not nearly as interesting as the person who eventually left.

The garage in the photo below would seem distinctly run-of-the-mill if Steve Jobs weren't standing in front or if a historic plaque did not proclaim it as the birthplace of Silicon Valley. The garages featured here are important because they are birthplaces to the 20th century as we knew it. Notable not because of their architecture, these structures are instead resonant with human curiosity, drive, excellence, and innovation.

The garage where Apple was born

It's suburban, stucco, and by all accounts just a garage. But with the founder of Apple computer standing out front, this modest two-car garage takes on a new shine. Four years after dropping out of his first semester at Reed College, Steve Jobs went home to his family in Los Altos, California. With the help of friend Steve Wozniak, Jobs determined to build a personal computer, which in 1976 was a revolutionary idea. (So revolutionary, in fact, that both Atari and Hewlett-Packard passed on the idea.)

The pair designed the Apple I in Jobs's bedroom and built the prototype in Jobs's garage. That computer, which looks like a boxy typewriter, had no monitor (you had to hook it up to your television) and sold for $666. The two made a reported $774,000 from its sale, then launched the Apple II. Within three years, the company grew by 700 percent, which catapulted Jobs and Wozniak firmly out of the garage.

These garages are important because they are birthplaces to the 20th century as we knew it.

Apple Computer founder Steve Jobs **stands in front of his parents' garage, the one he and partner Steve Wozniak retreated to when they were designing and building the Apple I computer.**

Walt Disney's small-world startup

There was a time when Walt Disney suffered for his art. His Kansas City animation business had gone bust and the situation looked bleak. So in 1923, Disney went to Hollywood, borrowed some money from his brother Roy, and set up shop in his uncle's garage (for rent of $1 a month).

Inside the garage, which Disney rented for $1 a month, the animation pioneer built a camera stand and shot a series of primitive cartoons that were to be shown in a vaudeville house.

Walt soon found a vaudeville house willing to sponsor some of his cartoons. He built a camera stand in the garage from wooden boxes and lumber, and started to draw. The cartoons, featuring primitive stick figures telling subtitled jokes, were followed by *Alice in Cartoonland,* Disney's first animated film. The Alice in Wonderlandish cartoon caught the attention of a New York producer, who ordered six more cartoons—this time at $1,500 each. The Walt Disney Co. began shortly thereafter, in a rented room behind a real estate office.

This humble garage was the temporary animation studio where Walt Disney began his cartoon career in California.

The *Reader's Digest* rental

This elegant garage in Pleasantville, New York, was not the birthplace of *Reader's Digest*. (A basement owns that claim.) But DeWitt and Lila Wallace moved here within a year of the first issue of *Reader's Digest*—an idea that came to Wallace, apparently after everything else (including copyediting and working as a ranch hand) failed to pan out.

The magazine's first issue was created in a basement apartment at 1 Minetta Lane in New York City. Subsequent issues were produced in a rented garage apartment in Pleasantville. By all accounts, the interior was pretty nice, featuring a fireplace and hardwood floors.

The idea that **DeWitt and Lila Wallace came up with was ingenious—to compile a grouping of magazine articles, edit them down carefully, and republish them as a digest. DeWitt and Lila borrowed $5,000 from his family to start the venture, and the early years of *Reader's Digest* were spent in this garage apartment.**

Attached, Detached, or Something In-Between?

*I*n the beginning, garages were out back, as far from the house as possible, because the flammable nature of the car and gasoline created a safety hazard. The garage moved closer to the house when fear over fire subsided and when the American passion for convenience found its expression in home design. From the 1940s on, the garage was more often than not attached to the house.

The attached garage

The attached garage has a number of advantages: avoidance of bad weather, placement of the kitchen near grocery delivery, and the convenience of other spaces in the garage close by. One immediate drawback is the loss of light on one side of the house; the garage sits, in other words, where windows might go.

And then there are the ugly attached garages: the ones that yawn in front of the house, in suburb after suburb, creating seas of suburban sameness. Nonetheless, attached garages can, with good design, be attractive extensions of the house.

The detached garage

It's generally true that most houses look better without a monolithic shed hanging off one side. And when a garage is detached, light can still enter the house from all four sides. Detached garages are versatile structures, often offering the best place to put a full-scale workshop, studio, home office, or guest house.

There's usually quite a bit of space to work with in a detached garage. The footprint of a minimum-sized two-car garage—20 ft. wide by 24 ft. deep—will give 480 sq. ft. on each floor, depending on how it's roofed.

The attached detached garage

There is one way to get the best of both the attached and detached worlds: build a detached garage and attach it to the house in any number of ways. The local climate will typically dictate the best approach to how this is done. For example, in a warm climate, a breezeway can create a covered walkway to the house from the garage. In a colder climate, the attachment can double as a mudroom.

This attached garage is designed **to function as an entrance and to match and complement the character and proportion of the house. It faces the street, but its doors are turned perpendicular, so that you don't see the garage door first.**

There's more light in a house **with a detached garage because windows bring light in on all four sides.**

Today's Garage

Whether it's attached or not, the garage offers the opportunity for home renovation. Putting the garage near or in the house offers room to grow. With its location outside the kitchen, the garage can be transformed into a bigger kitchen or into a family room. There's also room for expansion above the garage—it's often an easy way to add a home office or a new master-bedroom suite.

For people with the urge to build but without an enormous budget, the garage is an opportunity to construct something smaller than a house but bigger than a shed, which can hold things the house or the shed can't or shouldn't. The garage can also come first in a long-term building project. In fact, it can even serve as a starter home—a place to live and park and eventually grow out of, leaving a guest house or an office space on the property.

The garage is bigger than ever. That may be because everything that goes in the garage is bigger.

Framed through the portico of the main house, this new garage is referred to as a "carriage house" and is used to house cars, tractors, and other equipment for the maintenance of a large estate; it's also got an additional five bays of storage at the back.

The era of the big garage

The garage is bigger than ever. That may be because everything that goes in the garage is bigger. Consider the growth of the American car. In 1917, the Model T measured a diminutive 138 in. Forty years later, the Lincoln is 6 ft. longer! The Ford Expedition, one of the more popular SUVs now on the road, is a whopping 205 in. long.

Needless to say, new cars don't fit in old garages. Not only that, sometime in the 1960s, families who owned one car now found two to be a necessity. Although the typical American house still came with the same series of rooms that it had for decades, the typical American family had undergone radical changes. Women entered the workforce, and teenagers gained an unprecedented amount of freedom and access to the car keys. Old garages were now almost entirely useless, except for storing the lawn-mower, which itself had grown much bigger.

So the garage got bigger. And it's still getting bigger. And bigger. By the 1990s, the nearly ubiquitous three-car garage—at least in places like California, Florida, Arizona, and Texas—had been superseded by a standard four- or five-car model. Not only is there need for a space that holds more vehicles, but the desire for overflow storage for any number of things provides the inspiration for garages with several bays and multiple functions.

Basketball star Shaquille O'Neal once owned a house in Florida with a 5,000-sq.-ft.

garage that included a movie theater, two bathrooms, a lounge, and room for 10 cars. Jay Leno, comedian and host of *The Tonight Show*, has an even bigger garage—measuring in at 44,000 sq. ft. That's the size of Bill Gates's entire house. Yet Gates's garage is no shrinking violet either. It holds 20 cars underground and doubles as a ballroom. Yet these mega-garages are actually no bigger than the stables at Versailles, which could hold 200 coaches and 2,400 horses.

Even normal people have big garages

As for those mega-garages that don't belong to royalty of one type or another, they constitute about 16 percent of the garages being built today. An Internet search for real estate in my area reveals 357 listings for homes with four or more car garages. A local boat tour of estates on a large lake near Minneapolis stops to point out a 12-car garage as if it were a tourist attraction. In Arizona, where the need for car space exceeds even California's, the local paper recently described a "14-car garage with remote-controlled turntable"—a sort of lazy Susan for cars.

The suburban streetscape of my childhood looks downright old-fashioned in comparison to today's luxurbia. Those garages of yesteryear, which were attached to 1950s ranch houses, were at the back of the house and down a long driveway. Big garages, up front, make the garage door a significant part of the front facade and give the house a big blank face. Whole streets—subdivisions even—of them create a sea of suburban sameness.

Suburban developments often put the garage **in front of the house. This creates streetscapes composed primarily of garages. And when the garages are unattractive, or even just bland, it can alter the whole perception of community: from a place where people live to a place where cars park.**

LOOK HOW THEY'VE GROWN

In 1917, the Model T measured about 11½ ft. bumper to bumper. Forty years later, anybody who tried to fit a Lincoln Continental in a Model T garage got a shock: the last 6 ft. of it wouldn't fit.

1917 Ford Model T
◄— 11 ft. 6 in. —►

◄——— 17 ft. 6 in. ———►
1957 Lincoln Continental

At Seaside, a planned community in Florida, streetscapes are designed to resemble a traditional, old-fashioned neighborhood, which means porches out front and garages placed in alleys.

A new, old-fashioned garage

A few forward-thinking developers and architects are reconsidering the typical suburban placement of the garage. Such consideration is part of a much larger rethinking of American community development called New Urbanism. The tenets of New Urbanism call for a return to some old-fashioned ideas, among them the position of the garage on the back alley.

Architects Andres Duany and Elizabeth Plater-Zyberk wrote about garage placement in an issue of *Wilson Quarterly:*

"While suburban developments have a variety of pleasant features—attractive landscaping, tidiness, compatible colors—they fail miserably at the vital task of being interesting. The reason in this case is that the only information these houses put forth to passersby is that cars live there. That may give cars a nice feeling, but it does not do much for people."

Duany and Plater-Zyberk belong to a growing group of American architects and planners who are creating suburban developments that replace the emphasis on automobiles with a nostalgia for the way neighborhoods used to work. At Seaside, a planned community in Florida, porches, sidewalks, and parks are designed back

New thinking in urban design in the Midwest also puts the porch out front (left) and the garage out back (above). This development offers garages that are designed for cars and for the interests of the people who live there.

into the neighborhood. The functions of a community—living, shopping, and recreation—are close together. And service alleys allow garages to hide their faces from the street.

As proponents for taking the garage away from the front of the house, these architects also believe that there's no better place for getting down to work, or play. Their latest design for a development on the outskirts of Madison, Wisconsin, features garages that are designed to accommodate cars as well as the interests of the family. The garages in Middleton Hills contain conservatories, mother-in-law apartments, studios, and cars.

The tenets of New Urbanism call for a return to some old-fashioned ideas, among them the position of the garage on the back alley.

This log-cabin garage, built entirely from recycled materials, is well suited to its nearby log-cabin house and a larger log-cabin garage apartment.

The stylish garage

After decades of drab, generic design, the garage is finally getting stylish again. New garage architecture is about matching the style of the house or having the garage express its own style. Log cabins beget log-cabin garages, modernist mansions meet modernist garages, and so forth.

But garage style is more than sheer good looks. Garage style is about making the garage useful for purposes other than just storing cars. Garage style means maximizing the space and potential of that little place at the end of the driveway. Garage style expresses personality—and it does it with the skills of good design or with sheer wit, ingenuity, or eccentricity. There's a home in southwestern Wisconsin notable not only for its Swedish influence but also for its garage, which is crowned by an outdoor gazebo. Accessible by a ladder, it offers views and a favorite spot for family picnics (see p. 104). That's garage style.

Architects designing new homes often create garages that match the design of the house and also offer extra useful space. For the homeowner, a spiffy garage means cheaper space than the more expensive square-foot cost for the rest of the house. Sometimes the space provides room to grow into; in some instances garages are finished with such detail that they become architectural statements unto themselves.

Architect David Salmela is making a name for himself designing houses and ingenious garages (see the photo on p. 28). These garages make architectural

After decades of drab, generic design, the garage is finally getting stylish again.

His and Hers parking spots **in Arkansas City, Kansas, express the eccentricity of garages, American-style.**

statements, and they also offer workshop space or room for guests. Such garages are taking garage design full circle—back to the days when parking the car was something elegant and worthy of the finely crafted automobile. These garages are part of the architecture of the house, yet they aren't simply camouflaged into the house's design. Sometimes they actually define it.

What Do We Do in the Garage?

The garage is a stage, complete with a mechanical curtain, and it rises on any number of scenes, all of which are directed by the passions, dreams, and interests of the people who choose to occupy it. When it's closed, the garage remains an enigma—sometimes stylish, certainly, but also blank. With the door open, the garage gives us a glimpse of something that is essential to the American way of life. And that boils down to basically any activity that doesn't fit in the house.

The garage has a dark side, which has something to do with the privacy it offers from the house. From pipe bombs to serial killings,

As a magnificent entrance **to the house, this garage creates a sense of progression and entry; it is also integral to the design of the house. Parking and workshop space are available on either side.**

crimes committed in garages could be the subject of another, less cheerful book. While researching this book, I heard more than one story that dealt with death, including a gothic tale set in a Midwestern garage of a murder-suicide involving two dentists, a lovely widow, a letter opener, and a noose.

The garage is another world down the driveway, and we go there to work, to play, sometimes to live, and almost always to park. The garage is the domain of the tinkerer, an office for the inventor, a stage for the musician, a potting shed for the gardener, a control center for a fledgling business, a display case for the car collector, and the perfect home office that comes *sans* commute.

Of course, the real garage aficionado takes play and work one step further and simply moves into the garage lock, stock, and barrel, where the lifestyle can be as rustic or elegant as the garage that inspires it. Living in the garage is not a new idea. In the 1920s, young couples could buy a "newlywed cottage" that had room for the car as well as space for them but not much more. The cottage was designed to evolve, eventually, into a full-time garage and work-

The place where fire engines **used to park has been transformed into a boat restoration studio.**

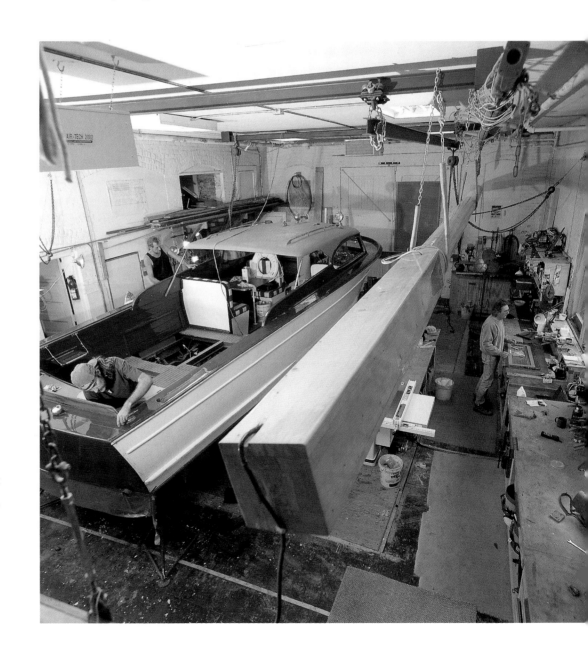

The garage is another world down the driveway, and we go there to work, to play, sometimes to live, and almost always to park.

TALES OF THE SUBURBAN GARAGE

*I*n recent times, the garage has become synonymous with suburbs, and filmmakers, writers, and other artists who address suburban angst in their work often look to the garage as if it's the apex of everything negative about suburban life. The suburb was after all made manifest by the car, and the garage is where those cars live.

Edward Scissorhands, Tim Burton's fairy tale set in the suburbs, casts the neighborhood in a colorful, cartoonish glow. In *American Beauty*, the Oscar-winning film from 1999, Lester Burnham, played by Kevin Spacey, retreats to the garage as an escape from his family. And in the television show *The Simpsons,* Homer's garage makes a frequent appearance and is referred to in one episode as "the car hole."

David Byrne in his film *True Stories* escorts us past row after row after row of matching suburban homes, their garage doors gleaming like teeth. We're so accustomed to seeing this scene as a kind of poster child for the soulless American way of life, that it surprises us when Byrne turns to the camera and asks, "Who's to say that this isn't beautiful?"

The suburbs—and the ever-important garage—is the setting for many tales of contemporary angst.

The advantages of the garage as home office: privacy, combined with proximity to the house, and a 20-second commute. This garage functions as office space for an architect.

shop, as the couple's finances increased and they were able to build a proper home on the property.

There are people who fantasize about their dream house. And then there are people who dream about the perfect garage. This book is for them, because people who dream about the garage tend to do things and to need places in which to do these things. This book shows you how to create a garage space that is efficient and stylish, a place to do what you like to do. In the following pages, you will see garage workshops, garage museums, garage apartments, garage pavilions, garage greenhouses, garage offices, garage libraries, garage studios, and just plain car garages. Maybe what the owners of these garages have discovered is a new kind of house, with two distinct parts—one where we sleep and cook and the other where we do everything else. ◆

It isn't much to look at, but this ordinary-looking garage is proof garage living is not a new idea. This "honeymoon house garage" from a 1916 issue of *Sunset* magazine would be the "home of a bride and groom while saving money to build a bigger nest and to buy an auto."

Shops & *Studios*

ARTIST MICHAEL MCMILLEN'S re-creation of a garage workshop is part of the permanent collection of the Los Angeles County Museum of Art. Cluttered with the bits and pieces of life, McMillen's installation combines worn tools, license plates, World War II memorabilia, old dentures, and screen doors. The shell of a Dodge Dart sits on a platform. Somehow, this "garage," very far removed from any sort of driveway, expresses a nostalgia for a generation of garage tinkerers who spent their free time in pursuit of the solitary pleasure that workspace gives.

While plenty of people insist that the basement is the only place for the workbench, the garage is the superior spot. It has windows, a door big enough to move projects and tools both in and out, instant ventilation, and the advantage of usually being removed from the laundry.

The 1950s *Popular Mechanics* book *How to Build Your Own Garage*, by Wayne Charles Leckey, counsels careful consideration of a

Artist Michael McMillen's installation in the Los Angeles County Museum of Art evokes a garage workshop brought to life, with all the detritus and clutter we associate with the garage, including a sculptural carcass of a vintage Dodge Dart.

This is the garage workshop/studio where Bob Smith maintains his collection of model trains and boats. The studio is climate-controlled to keep the collection safe from humidity.

workshop for your new garage: "If you like to make things, you'll surely want your garage plans to include a workshop...how pretentious this might be depends upon how enthusiastic you are about your pet hobby, how plump your pocketbook is, and how much yard space you have."

A more recent record shows the cost advantages to adding workspace to the garage: In 1999, it cost about $25 per square foot to add garage space. In contrast, it cost a minimum of $100 per square foot to add onto a house.

The garages featured in this chapter are in use as creative spaces, places where people with urges to make things go. As such, they often display

By building this garage **with premade attic trusses, the owners created a second-story space that can immediately be used for storage and offers the potential to become a finished room in the future.**

creative solutions to space and organization issues. If you've ever wanted space within the house to work on something other than the basic functions of living, a look at the following pages will convince you that the garage is that place. These garages, which range from a funky rented garage in a poor neighborhood in Washington, D.C., to the garage studio of professional furniture maker Thomas Moser, are testaments to human curiosity, creativity, and invention. ✦

The Hand-Built Garage

Clyde Kennedy's first garage took him 11 days to build and cost $300.

CLYDE KENNEDY BUILT HIS first garage back in 1949. It measured a diminutive 12 ft. by 12 ft., had a dirt floor, handmade garage doors, and a tar-paper roof, and was entirely constructed from concrete block. It took him 11 days to build and cost $300. When a neighbor noticed the workmanship, he asked Kennedy to build him a garage. Kennedy charged $600 for the neighbor's garage, which he and his wife spent on a television set, a move he now reckons "was a terrible mistake."

The two garages that sit on his property in southern Ohio are perhaps the antithesis to those he built 50 years ago. Constructed entirely

THE ADAPTABLE GARAGE

If a new garage will one day serve as a workshop, it should be conceived and designed as a workshop from the start. The same principle applies for a new garage that might see eventual duty as a guest house. Whatever the ultimate—or even likely—use of the garage, it should be reflected in the design and construction.

For instance, if a one-story garage will become a two-story garage sometime in the future, the original foundation should be able to support the extra weight of the additional story. Ordinarily, the ceiling joists in a simple one-story garage would be made of 2x4s; but if a second floor is likely, heavier ceiling joists will be needed. The same goes for wiring and plumbing: If there are expansion plans for a garage, it's a lot cheaper to plumb it and wire it for future uses when it is built.

BUILD IN ROOM FOR THE FUTURE

Standard roof truss leaves little room upstairs.

Attic roof truss provides potential space for later use.

Scissor roof truss offers vaulted upstairs space.

From the "carport's" front porch, **a view of the Kennedys' log-cabin house and garage, which was built to really park the vehicles, set within the rolling landscape of southern Ohio.**

Clyde and Dawn built a garage and still didn't have a place to park their cars.

from recycled wood and other materials, these two garages are what Kennedy himself calls "the last hurrah" of his multifaceted career as an artist and builder.

Kennedy started the first of the two new garages after completing a log-cabin retirement home for himself and his wife, Dawn. It wasn't too long after the cabin was completed that he embarked on the garage that he modestly calls the "carport."

Figuring it out as they go

Clyde and Dawn started building that carport about 200 ft. from the cabin. The Kennedys build the way many early master builders did—entirely by eye, sizing up the day's work and then determining as they go "if it looks good."

At some point Clyde decided the simple carport should have a second level, which would become his art studio; his workshop would be downstairs. And at any time, the two-story garage could be converted into a sort of mother-in-law apartment. "We decided to go ahead and put wiring downstairs, and then I could have the shop out there, but the wiring could also be laid out for a kitchen. I just told Dawn, we might as well make it so that if someone wanted to make it into living quarters, they could." No one has actually slept in it yet, but Kennedy swears if his wife wants him out of the house, all he'll need is a cot.

Reaching into the past

The "carport" is built, like most of Kennedy's structures, entirely from recycled materials. An old barn, falling down from neglect, provided the slate roof and the siding; the windows came from an old schoolhouse and the red-oak flooring inside from a relative's going-out-of-business sale. The stairs that lead from the workshop to the studio (where Clyde goes to paint and to

write an autobiography that's been stewing for about 30 years) were salvaged from an old house.

So Clyde and Dawn built a garage and still didn't have a place to park their cars. About 12 years ago, he started building what would definitely become the car garage. And he put this one closer to the house, remembering the advice given to him by an elderly uncle: "Think wheelchair, Clyde, whenever you're building." This garage is on the same level as his home's main entrance, a leveling feat that required 30 tons of fill. Again, this one was built with all recycled materials, even the reinforcing steel for the foundation came from an old bridge that was being replaced.

The property contained a circa 1820 log cabin, which Kennedy dismantled, refashioning the logs into the garage. Kennedy finished the log garage with a slate roof, lightning rods (all salvaged), and seven little slits in the log chinking that contain copper screen. Kennedy calls them gun ports; his wife considers them useful ventilation. ✦

In a quest for parking space, **Clyde Kennedy built two garages over the span of a decade. The first, which has become all workshop and studio space, began with every intention of being parkable space. Hand built by Kennedy and his wife, Dawn, the garage features entirely recycled materials, including an iron railing and a front porch.**

The upper level of the garage **is where Clyde Kennedy works on his painting and his writing. Trained as an artist, Kennedy spent most of his career in the building trade. Now retired, the projects he undertakes are primarily new structures and furniture for his log-cabin home.**

A Model Garage

BOB SMITH, A BUILDER BY TRADE and a model builder and train collector by hobby, had outgrown all possible alternatives his house offered for extra space: a spare bedroom and the basement. So Smith determined to build a multifunctional building where he could park, work on his model train and boat collection, and store tools for his business.

In designing the structure, Smith looked far from his Kentucky setting to New England for inspiration. The clapboard-sided garage features a cupola-topped gateway, which marks the entrance to the house with an East Coast flair. But rather than build one large building, Smith divided the various functions into separate buildings: one contains a workshop, the other is a model-building studio that also holds a collection of old model trains. Smith needed the storage, but he knew that the intricate boat models he builds were worthy of display. In effect, he created a small showplace for his collection that is climate-controlled to protect them from humidity and heat.

The cupola, which crowns the porte cochere between the two buildings, is made from recycled windows and serves as decoration and also as a vent for what Smith calls an "upstairs basement," or upper-level loft storage.

Bob Smith built this garage **with the idea that it would be a workshop and a place for his model-train and boat collection to be built and stored. It's designed to function as a back entrance to the yard, with a gate, porte cochere, and cupola marking the entranceway.**

Surrounded by patio space, the two wings of the garage workshop
separate the model-building studio from the owner's tool-storage area.

Smith's interest in boats and trains goes back to his childhood model train that was set up in his parents' basement. His current collection, primarily pre- and postwar Lionel steam engines, now numbers more than 100, all of which are stored in the climate-controlled building. The rest of the model studio is dedicated to building model boats, an interest that taps into Smith's fascination with maritime history. (When Smith builds a model boat, he restricts himself to ships that played an important part in American history.)

Once a year, starting at Thanksgiving, Smith lays track for the trains to travel to the house and throughout all four levels. "I try to limit myself to one period of insanity during the holiday season," says Smith. ◆

The workshop space **is divided between the owner's two passions— trains and boats. The shelves contain his premier collection of O- and G-gauge Lionel steam engines. The boats are painstakingly researched and built by hand to commemorate famous vessels from American maritime history.**

Boats in a Firehouse

KNOWN TO THE neighborhood as Fire Station No. 21, this 1910 building is now the home of Shipwrights, Inc., possibly the finest boat-restoration business in the upper Midwest, and the living space and workspace of Mark Sauer and Petronella Ytsma, boatbuilder and professional photographer, respectively.

The building ceased to be a fire station in the mid-1940s, serving various neighborhood roles over the years, among them VFW outpost and gymnasium. By the time Mark and Petronella purchased the building, it was both in a state of disrepair and covered in layers of badly done repair. It was a building inspector, faced with the unenviable task of describing the new use for the station, who came up with the term of "home with tuck-under garage." "Which is exactly what it is. Except for the fact that it's almost 6,000 sq. ft. and there's a brick turret," Petronella admits.

That tuck-under garage, once home to two fire engines, is now the couple's workspace. A shooting studio for Petronella's photography

The fire engine—size garage doors on this former fire station now make room for boats. In its latest incarnation, the 6,000-sq.-ft. building is workspace and living space for a boatbuilder and a professional photographer.

Design Challenges and Solutions

The challenges

+ Undo poor existing renovation
+ Convert fire-station bays into work-shop and photo studio
+ Create living space out of cavernous second floor
+ Make the building more livable

The solutions

+ Demolish old renovation and salvage usable materials
+ Restore main bay for use as boat-repair shop
+ Remodel rear rooms into a single 20-ft. by 26-ft. photo studio
+ Add windows upstairs and downstairs
+ Move kitchen into living space and separate with half-wall

business occupies the last 20 ft. of the garage, while the rest of it forms a 50-ft. by 26-ft. restoration bay, where Mark and his employees work on as many as six boats a year. With its high ceilings, insulated walls, and new windows carved into the west wall, the space could be any artist's studio. What gives it away are the oversized garage doors—once raised when a fire alarm rang, now to deliver boats for repair.

Upstairs, the barracks (which had also been a boxing club, a video store, and a meeting room for a German cultural society) still had a working kitchen and bath, which Petronella and Mark determined to retain as much as possible. Cabinets and the sink were salvaged. But the kitchen had been moved, so they relocated it to the living area, hiding it behind a half-wall that allows whoever is cooking to talk with guests. Two bedrooms were carved out of the front of the building and an office and darkroom space from the back. The renovation of the upstairs apartment was a five-year project complicated by numerous technical difficulties—among them, zoning laws, code restrictions, and

The boats that come to Shipwrights, Inc., range from the sublime Riva speedboat to the ridiculously beautiful 1925 Hackercraft motorboat. The former parking area for fire engines was a perfect space to restore boats. Here, Mark and crew are at work restoring a 1954 Chris Craft.

a cavernous space that demanded enormous amounts of sweat equity and materials.

On a recent open house, the couple invited the neighborhood to see their renovation. Among the visitors were four men in their late 70s who had worked in the station in the 1930s. "Each walked around, trying to remember where the pole had been," says Petronella. "And each took a corner and swore up and down that there's where it was." ✦

The area that served as barracks for firemen is now a loft living space. In the restoration, the kitchen was moved from the back of the building to the central area to connect it to the living space. Decay-resistant hardwoods like teak and mahogany, which Sauer uses in his restorations, were used to trim windows, doors, and kitchen counters.

It's safe to say that Hampton with his calling had no place else to go but the garage.

The Fear-Not Garage

IN 1950, JAMES HAMPTON, recently retired from his job as a janitor in a public school, rented an unheated garage in a poor neighborhood in the District of Columbia. For the next 14 years, he worked on his project, "The Throne of the Third Heaven of the Nations Millennium General Assembly." Using discarded materials like foil wrappers, old furniture, bottles, light bulbs, and plastic sheets, Hampton built an extraordinary, glittering sculpture, above which was a throne emblazoned with the words "Fear Not."

Hampton, who died right after completing his masterpiece, claimed to have been visited throughout his life by God and an assortment of His angels. He looked to God as his supervisor on the Throne project, and believed that the Lord visited the garage often in that capacity—and to dictate certain words, which are found written throughout the installation.

Hampton's sister came to Washington when her brother died. While cleaning up his effects, she literally raised the garage door and saw her brother's work for the first time. Luckily, the garage's owner wanted to save Hampton's work; ultimately, it was acquired by the Smithsonian and is now part of its permanent collection. It's safe to say that Hampton with his calling had no place else to go but the garage. ✦

Retired janitor James Hampton rented a garage to construct an elaborate, glittering throne, which he dedicated to the heavens. The contents of the garage are now part of the Smithsonian's collection of American art.

Thomas Moser's Workshop: A Tinkerer's Dream

THOMAS MOSER'S FURNITURE DESIGN, which is influenced by Shaker and Arts and Crafts styles, is notable for its singularity, for its craft, and for the timelessness of its forms. His business, Thomas Moser Cabinets, is known worldwide and has grown since 1973 to occupy a 65,000-sq.-ft. work-space in Maine and showrooms across the country.

The house where Thomas Moser and his wife Mary live is notable also for its design and for its craft, as well as for the extraordinary piece of land it occupies. Their unique location on an island off the Maine coast was for almost 100 years the site of the local ice house. Before the advent of refrigeration, ice was made from a nearby freshwater source and then transported to other small towns on the salt water.

In the design of his home workshop and garage, Moser looked to the original ice house for inspiration. The exterior of the structure, which holds a garage, a studio for large wooden boats, and an apartment and workshop, is classic New England—restrained, shingled, and faded by weather.

Thomas Moser designed **a multi-functional structure that can alternatively be used as a place for boat restoration, a guest house, his personal workshop, and a garage.**

In the design of his home workshop and garage, Moser looked to the original ice house for inspiration.

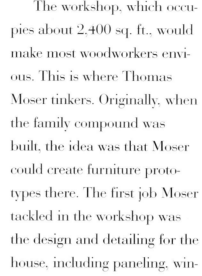

The workshop, which occupies about 2,400 sq. ft., would make most woodworkers envious. This is where Thomas Moser tinkers. Originally, when the family compound was built, the idea was that Moser could create furniture prototypes there. The first job Moser tackled in the workshop was the design and detailing for the house, including paneling, windows, and doors. Thomas's son, David, who now does much of the design work for the company, has also used the workshop in the design of his own house, just yards away.

Designed to have plenty of light, the shop holds an immense number of tools and, with its cathedral ceiling, gives the tinkerer a spatial sense of extravagance. The workspace is often in use for boat restoration: currently in the works is the dismantling of a 16-ft. Century, which is being taken apart systematically, each part numbered and used as a template, to create a boat nearly identical to the original.

The garage function of the building has been more minimal, admits David, especially in the summer months, because the boat restoration consumes the parking bays. Even with a boat in the works, the structure manages to hold a tractor and a motorcycle. ◆

This workshop is a tinkerer's dream, **as well crafted as a piece of Thomas Moser furniture. The garage workshop is in service to what David Moser calls "esoteric tinkering," as well as wooden boat restoration and various building and restoration projects.**

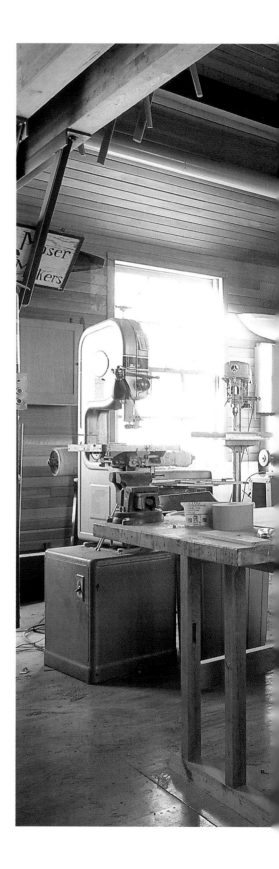

This garage studio measures **the full width of a city lot yet doesn't dominate the backyard because of the presence of the garden. Shuttered windows enliven what could have been a blank wall, and paved walkways make the garage the garden's ultimate destination.**

Their new garage studio spent about five years as essentially one big space that held two cars and a lot of clutter.

Ruling Principles: Economy and Space

WHEN LYNN WADSWORTH and David Amdur left Brooklyn for the Midwest, they entered a more sane real estate market, one where it seemed possible for the first time to own, not just to rent. Both Lynn and David are artists, and in Brooklyn they were accustomed to renting both living and studio space. But away from the stratospheric real-estate market of New York, they began to think about owning their own home and creating their own studio.

The Tudor-style house they purchased came with a less-than-charming 1920s garage, not suitable for cars or for studios. Calculating that the cost of building a structure would more than pay for itself in 10 years, given the relatively low figure of $200 a month to rent outside of the home, the couple determined that the best place to put the studio would be in a new garage.

The garage they built was ruled by the principles of economy and space; for under $20,000, they built a heated, insulated structure that's become a place where they park, work, and occasionally hold art classes.

Lynn is the first to admit that their new garage studio spent about five years as essentially one big space that held two cars and a lot of clutter. Both the clutter and the presence of the car proved to be dis-

A simple interior gives the artists space **for material storage. An old library table in the center of the room is the primary workspace. On the other side of the French doors is a jumble of garage storage.**

ruptive to the creative process, and the expanse of space felt overwhelming. French doors, discovered in the basement, became a clever, inexpensive way to demarcate space.

Adding an interior window helped allow the light from the exterior window inside. Now with functions clearly separated between parking and studio space, the garage is fully functional as a ceramic studio where Lynn creates beautiful hand-carved tiles and David works on his oil paintings. ✦

The owners came up with **an ingenious and inexpensive way to separate the parking and storage area from the workspace: Old French doors and a small window, salvaged from a house in the neighborhood, mark the barrier. Inside, artist Lynn Wadsworth is at work making ceramic tiles.**

Transformed from a garage into a workshop, where projects from a hand-built kayak to a theatrical set piece might be undertaken, this garage sits in the middle of the backyard. Its owners have made every effort to integrate it into the garden, with trellises, climbing plants, and a nearby deck; the driveway makes for a good patio.

Workshop in the Garden

To ROSE RIORDAN AND CREON THORNE, one of the best things about their 1920s bungalow was the garage. The house needed work and the garden had potential, but the garage that sat in the middle of the backyard had workshop written all over it. It ceased to even be a garage in the usual sense of the word the minute they moved in; the driveway became a patio and the garage's interior was taken over by a professional-level woodshop, which Creon uses to build furniture and set pieces for various theatrical productions.

What had been the driveway was easily converted into a patio, with a fence fully enclosing the yard. In fact, with the driveway so close to the house, it had effectively severed the house from the garden. By relandscaping so that the small yard offers sitting areas as well as lush borders, the garage is now at home in the garden. To integrate the garage's exterior with its garden setting, the couple placed trellises and vines over the entrance. ✦

All available space has been dedicated to work. A workbench in the corner, plenty of metal shelving, and storage of kayak forms on the ceiling make the most of a small amount of workspace.

> *The house and the garage are influenced by a Japanese aesthetic, marked by hand-hewn beams, wide eaves, and a tile roof.*

The garage that builder **Louis McBride designed and built in northern California is influenced by a Japanese aesthetic: The doors duplicate a Japanese *shoji* screen, and the wide eaves and tile-covered pergola walkway create an elegant compound.**

Shoji Studio

KATHERINE BAYZAK COMMUTES TO A high school where she teaches painting. For her own studio, she wanted a place a bit closer to home. That place is a garage, designed to stylistically match a home that she and her husband built on five acres in northern California.

The house and the garage are influenced by a Japanese aesthetic, marked by hand-hewn beams, wide eaves, and a tile roof. For the interior, Bayzak was interested less in aesthetics than in practicality and budget. The light in northern California can be strong, which can be detrimental to artists who need more controlled light. So the windows are small and primarily face north, where they are shaded by the garage's wide eaves. Inside, the studio has a floor of unfinished plywood and walls of unadorned drywall. Rafters are exposed and give the space a vaulted ceiling.

While the studio area is Bayzak's domain, she and her husband use the rest of the garage for an annual Super Bowl party. "We literally roll out the carpet, take the cars out, and invite all our friends and neighbors. The garage is as nice as the house," says Bayzak.

The garage is attached to the house with a pergola-covered walkway, which also extends the design aesthetic. "We didn't want it to look so garagy," says Katherine. And the garage doors offer a beautiful finishing detail that's important to the overall architecture of the compound. The first idea was to use *shoji* screens, made from Japanese rice paper and balsa wood, which would have been entirely impractical in any kind of weather other than mild and sunny. To duplicate the look and create a weather-resistant door, builder Louis McBride came up with the idea of pressing fiberglass paper between panes of glass. ◆

The garage is joined to the house with a multilevel walkway that creates an elegant sense of arrival. It also extends the house and creates a strong visual connection that ties the house with the garage.

Inside and upstairs, the garage becomes an artist's studio. **Created with a minimum of means, this studio features plywood floors and exposed rafters.**

Design Challenges and Solutions

The challenges

+ Create a garage/studio that matches house style
+ Tie building to house
+ Garage doors that fit Japanese influence

The solutions

+ Build low eaves and exposed rafters to mimic house detailing
+ Construct covered walkway that matches garage and house
+ Build garage-door windows with fiberglass paper between panes to simulate *shoji* screens

Louis Windhorn's garage workshop is mostly workshop. The garage part, right near the front entrance, kept the car (back then a Model T), while the rest of the structure was dedicated to his neon-sign business.

Signs of the Times

If THE NEON SIGNS LOUIS WINDHORN MADE for the city of New Ulm, Minnesota, were to be lined up end to end, they'd stretch out for three miles. From 1930 until his death in 1975, every brewery, root-beer stand, and restaurant in this small Midwestern town boasted a Windhorn neon sign.

Windhorn's sign shop and garage studio are now empty, but even 20 years later, faded and chipped, the faux-painted walls and ceiling, the bamboo archways, and elaborate 3-D neon paintings that adorn the space pay tribute to a man who clearly had some strong creative urges.

The garage workspace is connected to the house via an underground tunnel that leads from the home's basement to the lower level of the garage, where Windhorn ran an importing business. The upper level held both his neon studio and his Ford. To call the space a garage workshop is probably giving too much prominence to what is mostly a workshop that included a parking space. Here, he worked with neon—an invention of the 1920s—embracing it with creative abandon, fashioning signs, nativity scenes, paintings, and interior lighting. Most of the equipment was against the wall, with work tables (also made by Windhorn) in the middle; during the weekends, the studio became the place for entertaining friends, neighbors, and fellow Masons.

On the lower level, Windhorn displayed his self-portrait (in a Shriner's hat). The shelves were put to use displaying a collection of imported brass, which Windhorn peddled just after World War II.

The neon studio, which Windhorn freely decorated, has been lovingly preserved
by some of his New Ulm neighbors. Strips of neon lights are attached to the ceiling beams; several of
Windhorn's neon-and-oil paintings are on display, including a landscape in the far corner.

An elaborate Indian-inspired screen made of a variety of materials marks the entrance to the workshop's lower level.

The garage workspace is connected to the house via an underground tunnel from the home's basement.

Windhorn referred to this room as "The Party Palace." It's attached—almost like a front porch—to another garage, which is next to the original. Windhorn acquired it after he had completely taken over the original garage as workspace.

Windhorn eventually acquired the garage next door. And with the notion that another garage would make room for more of his singular decorations, he added on what he called "The Party Palace," a porch-like room with a bar promising that "troubles end here."

The Windhorn property has been lovingly maintained as a kind of museum by neighbors Sid and Jan DeLeo, who also run a sign shop out of their garage. While the DeLeo's business thrives in that garage, they look wistfully across the alley at Windhorn's garage. "That would make a great studio," says Jan DeLeo, "and we're going to try and be there soon." Windhorn's garage would give them not only more space but a connection to a bit of small-town history—and a work environment both strange and wonderful. ✦

ABOUT SKYLIGHTS AND ROOF WINDOWS

A skylight is considered the "poor man's dormer." While older skylights tend to be bubbles of Plexiglas that often leak water and heat, newer skylights offer the drama of sun or moonlight without those other drawbacks. Even better than a skylight in some cases is the roof window, which is essentially a window that works like a skylight but gives both views and ventilation. Usually installed in remodeled attics, they capture 30 percent more light than an ordinary window and, as opposed to skylights, are at eye level.

However, in a full second story (where you don't see the roof line) or in a cathedral ceiling, a skylight is what you want. And there are a few guidelines for maximizing the light from the skylight:

- ✦ For direct, focused light, the opening in the roof and ceiling should be the same size as the skylight.

- ✦ For more dispersed light, the ceiling opening should be flared like a funnel to spread out the rays of natural light.

- ✦ For dispersed light where the ceiling doesn't express the pitch of the roof (in other words, the ceiling is flat, not vaulted), the light well should be flared from skylight to ceiling.

It's important to keep in mind the location of the sun relative to the skylight or roof window. A skylight on the north side of a roof will only provide muted daylight, which would be ideal for a painter. But for stronger light, the skylight should go on the south-, east-, or west-facing side of the roof.

PLAYING WITH LIGHT

The opening in the roof will always be the size of the skylight, but the opening in the ceiling can be shaped to affect the light in a variety of ways.

Direct light

The light follows the opening of the skylight.

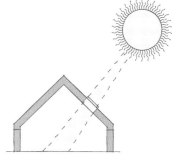

Dispersed light, vaulted ceiling

With a wider opening in the ceiling, the light gets dispersed throughout the room.

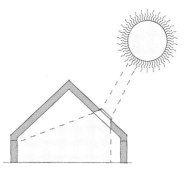

Dispersed light, flat ceiling

The light can be shaped, directed, and dispersed by the angle and size of the light shaft.

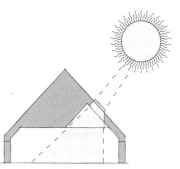

Taking Over the Backyard

S HE'S AN ARTIST AND HE'S A PHYSICIST; their daughter is an architect. Such alignment of professions resulted in a remodeled garage that creates space for a studio, a home office, and a patio for outside entertaining.

Her parents' Spanish-style bungalow did not give architect Claire Beasley much room to expand, except at the rear of the house, which was occupied by a one-car garage. That garage has been expanded and transformed into an artist's studio, while the rest of the backyard became room for a 10-ft. by 15-ft. home office and patio. There's still room for one enclosed parking space and off-street parking.

The studio and the office are separated by an exterior arcade, which connects the driveway with the back entry of the house. The rest of the remaining outdoor space was paved with bricks to become an outdoor room for entertaining, a space that the family uses frequently in this mild, bug-free climate.

The house has a distinctive Spanish style, and the architect was sensitive to it in the design of the addition, which boasts the same tile roof and arched doorways as the house. ✦

There's room to park **in this spacious artist's studio, but the mild California climate allows artist JoAnne Beasley to keep the car outdoors and claim most of the space for work. There's also plenty of natural light: French doors lead from the studio to an outdoor patio.**

A covered, Spanish-style arcade leads from the driveway to the rear entry of the house. The garage studio opens onto the brick patio and has two entrances.

The 10-ft. by 15-ft. office space is its own structure, connected to the home's back entrance with a covered arcade. The siting of the office, which takes over space once occupied by a patio, gives privacy to the new back courtyard by blocking views of the street.

The stone lion's head, inset into the board-and-batten wall that divides the two garage doors, was hand-carved by the builder's father, a Scottish stone mason.

The Tidiest Workshop in the World

THE INTERIOR OF THIS GARAGE, located in Vancouver, British Columbia, seems too spotless to be a workshop. The built-in cabinetry is suitable for a dining room, and the floor is of that well-known but seldom-found variety on which one could, if so inclined, eat. Although the lack of standard construction debris seems to belie the fact, John Farquhar, who has worked for many years as a finish carpenter, does indeed use the workshop—primarily for building cabinets but also for various jobs that can't be done on a building site.

The plan is simple: one big room. There's space for a car, and even more space to work with the car pulled out. There's an open space above, where Farquhar often stores building materials. The Prairie-style windows, essential for natural light during Vancouver's grayer months, were added because Farquhar couldn't resist the deal he got on them. The cabinets are made from maple, the builder's choice because of its hardness; they're stained a dark mahogany. And the floor, a marvel of

There's often no room for cars inside; the workshop area occupies the entire garage, if necessary, and the car gets pulled out to the driveway. The cabinets are furniture-quality, constructed from maple and stained a mahogany color.

shining concrete, got that way through extra time spent in the curing process followed by two layers of a hand-applied concrete sealer.

The lion plaque that adorns the exterior of the garage was made by Farquhar's father, who worked as a stone mason in Aberdeen, Scotland. Farquhar retrieved it three years ago and displayed it in the house until he found the right place to really show it off.

The garage sits on the same property as his house, where he was careful not to block views of the water. Hence the very low hipped roof, which breaks at just the right place to allow for a clear sightline of the bay from the house. ✦

There's space for a car, and even more space to work with the car pulled out.

This tidy little **Arts and Crafts–style garage was designed and built to function as a garage and workshop for a man who owns a small construction business in Vancouver, British Columbia.**

Ballou wanted the garage to look properly subordinate to the Victorian-style house yet to visually complement it.

The workshop inside **is filled with tools from another era. The owner is fascinated with nonelectrical machinery and uses a combination of old and new tools in the creation of his own work.**

Under the Victorian Influence

MICHAEL BALLOU AND HIS FAMILY moved to the Pacific Northwest after living 10 years in the wilds of northwestern Montana in a tepee. The Victorian-style house and garage they built is a perfect example, says Ballou, of the irony in John Lennon's lyric, "Life is what happens to you when your plans fall through."

The garage came after the house, prompted by a need for a workshop, which at various times was located in several places throughout the house, from the basement to the family room. Ballou purchased about 10 percent more material than he needed for the house, with the idea of using the leftovers for the garage.

Ballou wanted the garage to look properly subordinate to the Victorian-style house yet to visually complement it. The brackets, siding, window trim, and color are the same in both. The scale of the garage, which is 24 ft. square and one-and-a-half stories tall, is kept at a subsidiary level by one major design decision: Ballou determined that both house and garage would fit into the topography of the land. Rather than raze a small hill, he built the garage into the 9-ft.-high embankment.

The advantage to this siting is that both the garage area and the workshop area above can essentially be entered at

This Victorian-style garage is built into a 9-ft. embankment. Builder Michael Ballou wanted the house and garage to nestle into the site's rolling landscape.

Building into an embankment gives the second-level workshop an advantage: deliveries can be made directly into the workshop, without having to haul anything heavy up a flight of stairs.

grade, which is a major convenience to its owner, who can move heavy equipment and materials into the workshop without having to lug them up a set of stairs.

An open space filled with light

The interior of the workshop is designed to provide plenty of natural light. The center of the space is open to the roof, so that the gable-end windows and the windows in the long shed dormers on both sides bring in light. The cupola, which gives the garage a Victorian flare, also functions as a constant light source, bringing in light from every direction. Ballou painted it white and put two floodlights inside. "At night, it provides a moonlight effect" and allows him to avoid burning exterior lights. The cupola also has operable windows, so it functions as a vent.

The layout of the workshop is simple—essentially Ballou wanted lots of workbench space and a centrally located table saw. Many of Ballou's tools are vintage; in fact, as he describes it, "I have a huge respect and love for using woodworking machinery that uses the human body, that's nonelectrical." Ballou's working method is often to "start with a shaving horse and shave the form with a drawknife and then finish the project with a lathe and a table saw." The shop is overbuilt, in the sense that it's been wired and plumbed should there be a need to turn it into a mother-in-law apartment.

The garden shed, which attaches to the garage on the south side, was added as a sort of shed extension. With its own door, the shed can be accessed without having to enter the garage. ✦

Giving Old Stuff New Life

There are compelling practical and environmental reasons to re-use building materials, be they windows, doors, or lumber. On a less practical level, sentimental value often comes attached to something old or used, and if the thing is unique enough, it often provides a great starting point for a garage design.

The most common way of re-using materials is to find a window or a door and use it as it's always been used. Lumber can also be re-used: The garage/barn on pp. 162–163 was constructed primarily from material salvaged from an old barn from the Maine countryside. And Clyde Kennedy, whose two garages are featured on pp. 35–37, re-used rebar from bridges, slate from old barns, balconies from grand old hotels, and logs from tumbling-down log cabins.

A less common way to re-use materials is to give them an entirely different use. The architect Antoni Gaudí, whose whimsical, striking buildings adorn Barcelona, used broken plates to create mosaic patterns on the exterior of his structures. The artist James Hampton, who worked in a rented garage, made beauty out of trash (see p. 44).

Recycled building materials **can add a touch of beauty and grace to a garage, often at a fraction of the cost of new materials. In this case, wainscoting, molding, and corner blocks were salvaged from a demolished bank in Axtel, Kansas.**

Garage *Ventures*

WHATEVER THE NOTION, the prototype, the invention, or the vision, it usually finds its way to the building in the backyard. I'd love to make the argument that it's the garage that inspires inventions, but that might be elevating the garage into the romantic realm, which is not my purpose at all. At the very least, the garage seems to be one common denominator for a lot of people with upstart, or startup, ideas.

The garage has become essential to the story of corporate origin. A bit like a politician born in a log cabin, a company born in the garage bespeaks corporate grit, homespun roots, and a kind of honesty available only to the humble. The garage, by all accounts, is the birthplace of American ingenuity. Palo Alto and environs became Silicon Valley when David Packard rented a garage at 367 Addison Avenue; the likes of Apple Computer, the Walt Disney Co., and Medtronic also started in garages.

The reason so much has happened so close to the house is that the garage usually comes with low rent. We're familiar with the advantages of working at home: conference calls while wearing a bathrobe,

A glance will tell you that this is a garage; a closer look reveals that it's a florist shop. In fact, the interior is completely dedicated to flowers—that's why the car parks outside in the driveway.

Andre Harvey's garage offers an example of what happens when a passion turns to profit—not only does the garage contain the business of an artisan, it displays a collection of early farm vehicles.

There's no garage door, no driveway; yet, paradoxically, there is a garage-door opener.

Virtual Garage

The garage that *garage.com* occupies is virtual. There's no garage door, no driveway; yet, paradoxically, there is a garage-door opener. When entrepreneurs and potential venture capitalists log on to the Website, they can click on the garage-door icon and submit their business plans in a graphic "garage."

Since 1998, this venture-capital investment bank (whose motto is "We start up startups") has helped more than 60 technology startup companies raise more than $200 million in venture capital. *Garage.com* not only helps match entrepreneurs with investors but also assists with refining business models and assembling business teams. The company's name came from the wife of CEO Guy Kawasaki, who thought that the word "garage" helped capture the spirit of American enterprise, particularly in Silicon Valley.

A bit like a politician born in a log cabin, a company born in the garage bespeaks corporate grit, homespun roots, and a kind of honesty available only to the humble.

coffee in the kitchen, and a chance to fold laundry instead of engaging in a few minutes of office gossip. An office in the garage offers all that and a bit of distance, both psychological and physical, which creates separation between family and work. The garage office is often a separate structure from the house, and while part of it houses the cars, the rest of it can stretch into a spacious office.

The garages in this chapter are working garages, places with a purpose: some are significant because of their history, others offer ideas on how to incorporate a workspace into the home. And then there are a few garages where there's been no attempt to disguise their "garageness." It's the grease and the dust and the metal shavings that express the essence of the garage. These inventors' garages prove that inspiration doesn't need a high-rise.

A Ground-Level Office and Garage

ARCHITECT ROBERT GERLOFF went to the garage for office space because his wife needed the basement. Gerloff and his wife, Lynette Lamb, a writer and editor, are both in business for themselves. When they welcomed a child into their family, they were determined to add office space to the home so that they could spend time with their new child while continuing their careers.

Gerloff, who meets often with clients, "wanted to have space for meetings, without having to clean the whole house." Because there was no original garage on the property, the couple decided to design and build a garage that could provide space for both office and car. Originally, the plan was to put the office on top of the garage, but two factors—a zoning height limit for secondary structures and clients with mobility issues—inspired Gerloff to design an office and a garage on one level.

Gerloff made every effort to design a structure that would complement his 1901 Shingle Style home. Simple clapboard siding and a front porch at the garage/office entrance do this modestly and well. The garage and office together

Inside, the office functions with great efficiency. **The half-wall adds privacy and also doubles as a place to pin up drawings during meetings with clients. With its sage-green walls, mod carpeting, and honey-colored woodwork, the interior is a stylish showcase for Gerloff's ideas and a perfect small-scale example to show clients options for their own homes or offices.**

Design Challenges and Solutions

The challenges
- ✦ Provide office space for small architectural practice, one car, extra storage
- ✦ Have room to divide office space for separate functions
- ✦ Meet local zoning height restrictions

The solutions
- ✦ Build a low, 50-ft.-wide garage with clapboard siding and porch to match house style
- ✦ Add a partial wall in office for room to hang drawings, and separate computer from meeting area
- ✦ Create high ceiling to open up small office space
- ✦ Construct one-and-a-half-bay garage beside office to provide car and extra space

The treetop window lets in light while at the same time obscuring views of a neighbor's garage, which is only a few feet away.

occupy the width of the 50-ft. lot; the parking space is one-and-a-half stalls, one for the family car and the rest for storage.

The porch outside the office helps shade the interior from late afternoon sun and imparts a homey texture. While Gerloff's fantasy of sitting on the porch with clients to sketch and talk has not yet materialized, the porch does offer a spot for the couple to watch their daughter at play in the backyard. It also allows for a large western-facing window that might have let in too much light without shade from the low roof.

Inside, the 252-sq.-ft. office offers enough office space for Gerloff, a part-time employee, and visiting clients. Such versatility of space is achieved through careful planning. The high ceiling makes the space feel larger, while the horizontal trim band and the darker color on the walls conspire to make it also feel cozy. A partial wall that divides the space serves as a place to pin up drawings during meetings; it also creates a visual separation from both Gerloff's desk and the technology area of the office. The office manages to be both a private place to work and a good place to meet with clients.

Gerloff wanted the office to reflect the sort of architecture he likes to design. The interior, as he puts it, is "millwork intense." Windows were planned to let in light and a view of treetops (as opposed to the neighbor's garage). The sill of the deep-set picture window doubles as a bench.

Because architecture is a profession that generates a lot of paperwork, Gerloff took precautions to put a firewall between the car stall and the office. There is room to grow only by taking over one of the parking bays, but Gerloff is intent on keeping his business the size his garage office can accommodate. ◆

A GROUND-LEVEL OFFICE AND GARAGE

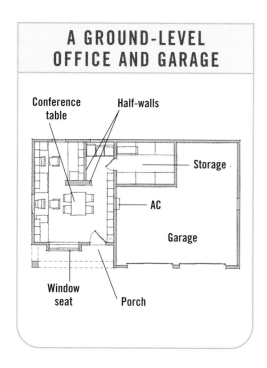

Conference table

Half-walls

Storage

AC

Garage

Window seat

Porch

The high ceiling makes the space feel larger, while the horizontal trim band and the darker color on the walls conspire to make it also feel cozy.

Half parking place, half office, this garage keeps everything on ground level. For architect Robert Gerloff, the one-story building allows him to comply with zoning height restrictions while making the office more accessible to clients with disabilities. The garage allots one space for parking the car, the other for parking bikes, trikes, and strollers.

The interior is designed to be flexible, thanks to pocket doors that allow space to be either sectioned off or opened up. While the garage now functions as an architect's home office, it could easily be converted into a guest cottage, with bathroom and changing facilities and easy access to the swimming pool.

Adaptable Office Space

FOR CALIFORNIA ARCHITECT KURT LAVENSON, a home isn't quite a home unless it has a separate office. So while searching for a new house, all prospective candidates had to offer the potential for office space apart from the house. Lavenson eventually settled on a modest ranch, which had just what he wanted: a simple two-car garage that also happened to be nestled under a magnificent oak tree. The garage had been used for tool storage and, because it was near a swimming pool, part of it had been converted into a small dressing room.

Lavenson first gutted the two-door garage down to the studs before starting to rebuild, revealing the beams on the ceiling, which created a 5-ft. grid. The plan adds a small tower at one end of the garage to hold equipment for the pool as well as heating and air-conditioning equipment for the new office.

The tree dictated the size of the addition, which involved building a new one-and-a-half-stall garage on the north side of the existing garage. The interior was divided into equal quadrants, using the 5-ft. grid provided by the ceiling beams—two for the home office, one for the bathroom and pool changing room, and one finished for possible use as a guest room or just a quiet place to get away. Lavenson

The tree dictated the size of the addition, which involved building a new one-and-a-half-stall garage on the north side of the existing garage.

Fitted with garage door—sized French doors in homage to the structure's original function, this poolside garage office also makes room inside for a changing area.

manipulates the space by using pocket doors, which he says offer privacy when closed and a larger, more spacious interior when opened.

Lavenson put the office on the garage's south side—toward the swimming pool, creating a kind of pool-house aesthetic by virtue of its position. Oversized French doors (which are so oversized they're the size of garage doors, in homage to the building's original function) connect the office with the outside.

Lavenson considered the open plan of the building essential to its future viability: "The space can play a lot of roles. It can easily be converted into a teenager's escape, a rental unit, or a home for elderly parents." ✦

Half of the garage is devoted **to office space. The desk and worktables that line the wall were designed and built by the architect.**

An Inventor's Garage

THERE ARE TWO WELL-WORN PATHS on Mark Zeh's garage floor—one that winds from the workbench to his Clausing metal-working drill press and the other to the attached kitchen, where Mark keeps the coffeepot. The rest of his garage, which is referred to by friends and patrons as the Zeh Industrial Complex, is a jumble of machinery, inventions, projects in progress, and posters of bike racers. This is a garage that Zeh is proud to admit "has never had a car in it."

For Zeh, who describes himself as a designer with a hands-on problem-solving approach, the garage has no equal as a workspace. The advantages—low rent, a 20-second commute, and the convenience of working whenever he feels like it—far outweigh what might be considered disadvantages, certainly by someone with a predilection for warmth and light.

Zeh began his career as an inventor in a basement shop, graduating to a garage when his first forays into the Cycle-Ops fluid bicycle trainer began to pay off. That first invention, which used a chamber filled with silicon fluid as a resistant, essentially revolutionized home-exercise equipment. Since then, he's gone on to design mechanisms for everything from toys to surgical tools.

On the day I visited him, Zeh claimed he had cleaned up the garage, which meant that some of the metal shavings were swept into a pile. The garage was filled with various projects—a custom-built bicycle frame, which he made out of scandium (a metal first used by the Soviet Union in the 1960s to build aircraft), and a prototype impact tester for a high-tech corporation. I asked Zeh if he ever dreamed of a bigger garage, perhaps one that could hold his truck as well. His response: "If I had more tools, then that might be necessary." ✦

This is a garage that Zeh is proud to admit "has never had a car in it."

Friends refer to Mark Zeh's workshop as the Zeh Industrial Complex, a name that somehow manages to capture the jungle of tools and inventions in this one-stall attached garage. Here, Zeh works with a Clausing industrial drill press.

Not only did this small garage restaurant flourish, it also garnered a four-star rating. The garage's advantage "was that it was there," say the owners. When the garage burned down in 1997, the Herbfarm Restaurant relocated to tonier surroundings, though it's still a favorite destination restaurant in the Seattle area.

As for putting the restaurant in the garage? "It was there," the owner says.

Four-Star Garage

THE HERBFARM RESTAURANT, a four-star destination in the Pacific Northwest, began when Lola Zimmerman took extra chive plants from her garden in Washington State and put them in a wheelbarrow by the road. She included a glass jar for honor-system payments. The plants sold and so the next year, she planted more herbs, with the idea that they might also sell. When they did, she and her husband determined to remodel the tractor shed as a place to buy and sell herbs.

Their son and daughter-in-law, Ron Zimmerman and Carrie Van Dyck, joined them in their venture a few years later, adding herb-based products and offering classes on herbs. In 1985, they built a garage: a standard, two-door version, with windows on the north side. They put picnic tables inside for visitors to the gardens to have their lunch.

As surely as those chive plants took root and grew, so too did the idea for a restaurant. "We were already offering a class that was a luncheon based on cooking with herbs," says Van Dyck. As for putting the restaurant in the garage? "It was there," she says.

The restaurant operated for just over 10 years in the garage: It seated 34 and, after a remodeling that added a bay window, 36 diners. The kitchen, small and admittedly cramped, was located in the back, where a workbench might typically go. In 1997, a fire destroyed the property and The Herbfarm moved out of the garage and off the farm to a new location in Woodinville, Washington.

The evolution of their garage from picnic spot to an elegantly appointed restaurant, where reservations must be made a year in advance, is a story as worthy of Horatio Alger as it is this book. The Herbfarm Restaurant began as a good idea matched with a good garage. ✦

Windows on the Garage

THE CREATION OF SOUND DEMANDS QUIET. And with two small children constantly in and out of the house on their way to the backyard, it became critical for a designer who has made a full-time business out of both sound and graphic design to find a place for peace and quiet. He decided that the quietest spot would be out of the house. A dilapidated garage sat out back, and the first idea was that "it would be cheaper to build on the original garage's existing foundation."

Which it would have been, except that he soon discovered that the existing garage had no foundation. Malcolm MacKenzie, an architect based in Newton, Massachusetts, designed a new structure, using the home's gambrel room and shingle cladding as inspiration. "The original house provided a great starting point," he says. "It's a gambrel-roofed house with fantastic windows. Both inspired the form of the garage."

The new garage that MacKenzie designed provides two parking spaces

The flying beams are structural and contribute to the quality of the interior space. A sitting area occupies one side of the office. The owner collects vintage signs, which are used throughout to add a strong visual element.

The great variety of windows was inspired by the house itself, which the architect speculates "must have been built nearly a hundred years ago by a window manufacturer." The crown molding that runs around the first level of the garage became window boxes for the stepped window pattern because the windows are pushed back. The door at the side of the garage is for direct access to garden equipment.

Clients can meet around a small table: There's no kitchen because local zoning laws prohibited space that might be considered livable, but a coffeepot and a sunny window make a good spot for coffee breaks.

The second story is full-sized and the gambrel roofline is finished off, leaving lots of variation in ceiling height from a full 16 ft. high in the center to nearly half that on the perimeter. It works well to create a sense of different spaces within one larger space. The office is divided into a few areas: The space that the designer needs to work is tucked into a corner.

and an upper-level office to the client; aesthetically, it is a witty counterpart to the house and is in total keeping with a neighborhood filled with two-story carriage houses.

The gambrel roofline, which matches the roof of the house, makes the garage look, on the outside, like a small building of note. Inside it creates a varied and interesting ceiling, which helps to define spaces within the one room.

The fenestration pattern that MacKenzie liked so much in the house inspired not only the number of windows (16) but also the great variety and patterning of them. The stepped window wall, which covers an interior stairway, faces the house; it's a striking use of windows—the window boxes are created from the crown molding on the garage, a detail that gives the garage tremendous personality. An oval window and elegant finishing details make this garage the Cadillac of the neighborhood. ◆

The entrance to this garage office is cleverly carved into a corner: two doors offer two options—one to the parking area, the other up a stairway illuminated by a stepped window pattern. A full two stories and 24 ft. square, the garage fits well into a neighborhood of older homes, many of which have carriage houses.

Shafer is sold on the garage — universally, he says, it's "the craftsman's cheapest place" to work.

Garage Cycle

Ross Shafer's first garage workshop was in Paradise, California. That was 24 years ago, in a funky little garage attached to the back of a cabin. Since then, Shafer has spent time in at least five different garages, among them his mother's—a basic suburban model, with a bench against the wall and power tools kept on the floor.

Shafer started building bikes in that first garage in 1976. Eventually, he developed his skills and his bikes into a nationally known bicycle company called Salsa Cycles, which employed 17 people in the service of building a better ride. Since recently selling the company to a national distributor, Shafer finds himself jobless but not garageless.

This man, who readily proclaims himself to be "gainfully self-unemployed," now spends most of his time in a corrugated tin-sided garage. It contains a sophisticated metalworking shop, where Shafer works primarily with stainless steel to craft objects ranging from vases to replacement parts for a collector of vintage racing motorcycles. These exact reproductions, crafted with exactitude, will become a visible part of this valuable motorcycle collection. Shafer has also taken on such projects as fabricating an electric bicycle for Ford Motor Co. and creating a table that features a built-in candelabra.

Shafer is sold on the garage—universally, he says, it's "the craftsman's cheapest place" to work. ◆

Although the garage is not large by any means, inventor and bike designer Ross Shafer finds room for the family MG. A basic and simple building, the exterior and roof are both clad in galvanized corrugated metal.

A garage for the "gainfully self-unemployed": **Sophisticated commercial metalworking equipment mixes with collected treasures, waiting to be transformed.**

Without the benefit of even an electric garage door, the Hewlett-Packard garage has become the quintessential startup garage.

The modest garage **at the end of the driveway is now considered the birthplace of Silicon Valley.**

Original Startup

MODEST, EVER-SO-SMALL at 12 ft. by 18 ft., and without the benefit of even an electric garage door, the Hewlett-Packard garage has become, in many ways, the quintessential garage, the one we think about when we think about garage startups. Even the California State Historical Landmarks has taken note, granting the modest wood-frame garage historic status and indicating it as the "birthplace of Silicon Valley."

The founders of the company, David Packard and William Hewlett, met when they were students at Stanford in the early 1930s. At the time, most Stanford graduates left California to work in the more established companies back East, which Packard briefly did. But after a few years at General Electric in Schenectady, New York, he returned to Palo Alto with the idea of starting a company with Hewlett.

In 1938, Packard and his wife rented the ground floor of a house that had a backyard with a cottage and garage. Hewlett was living in the cottage. The two went to the garage to work on quite a few electronic inventions, including a bowling-alley foul-line indicator and a harmonica tuner, before they turned their attention to what would be their breakthrough. Their resistance-tuned sound oscillator generated audio frequencies that were used to test sound equipment.

Perhaps their smartest move was to price the instrument low, at $54.40. With other oscillators going for about $400, they found themselves with a seller. Interestingly enough, an early order for the oscillators came from the Walt Disney Co., which used them for the production of the film *Fantasia*. (Disney himself had started his own venture in a garage.)

The two men were well on their way to creating a business. Needing a name for the business, they flipped a coin to see whose name went first, and Hewlett-Packard was officially born. Within a year, their sales topped $5,000, and the two men left the garage.

But the garage has never really left Hewlett-Packard. Lisa Carr, in charge of the garage image at HP, says the garage has been an essential image to the corporation because it embodies the spirit of invention. Integral to its identity and also to its internal culture, the garage has become emblematic of how HP is defining itself in the greater community. A prominent part of a recent international advertising campaign, the garage has been featured in print and TV ads shown around the world. ✦

This wooden structure, decorated only with a wreath of morning glories, is now featured in a series of HP advertisements that express the spirit of invention inherent in the garage.

Photogenic Garage

WHILE ERIC ROTH'S photographic skills take him around the country, the base of his operation is found just outside his Massachusetts home in a renovated building that combines the best of what garages and carriage houses can offer.

Originally designed with five working bays, the structure needed an enormous amount of renovation, which included gutting, reconstructing, replumbing, and rewiring. In the middle of the building, Roth knocked out the floor between the downstairs and upstairs, giving him a central workspace with a high ceiling, which he uses for photography shoots. The work area is defined by a kitchen on one end, which was necessary for food shoots, and a private reading nook that's big enough for some shelves and a plaid chair and ottoman. The second-level space is divided between a storage/darkroom area and an office.

This 60-ft.-long renovated carriage house originally had five parking stalls. The entire building has been converted to office space for its owner, a professional photographer, who uses the space for photo shoots, storage, and computer-based work. The cupola, outfitted with a fan, brings instant ventilation during hot weather.

The two-story central work area is used for in-house photo shoots, which include everything from food shots to vignettes for home-and-garden publications. The basketball hoop provides exercise; with a 40-ft. free-throw area, photographer Eric Roth can get in a good workout. The second-story level, which is an open loft on one side, is where Roth stores his negatives and keeps his darkroom.

Originally designed with five working bays, the structure needed an enormous amount of renovation, which included gutting, reconstructing, replumbing, and rewiring.

One of the owner's favorite areas is this reading nook, which is outfitted with shelves, an easy chair and ottoman, and favorite framed images.

Design Challenges and Solutions

The challenges

✦ Renovate a huge, dilapidated carriage house

✦ Create space for a working photo studio

✦ Include kitchen for food photography

✦ Design space that also functions as an office

The solutions

✦ Gut interior, rebuild, rewire, replumb

✦ Create two-story space with kitchen for photo studio

✦ Add nook for desk and shelves

✦ Use upper floor for darkroom and storage

The downstairs floors, which are new, cover ugly concrete. While they look old, Roth reports that they are the result of bargain hunting and stockpiling: "Whenever Home Depot had Classic Pine #4 in 12-in. boards, I'd buy them out and save it up. A lot of people cautioned against pine, but there's no problem at all—it does get dents, but I like dents," he says. ✦

Within the large converted carriage house is room for a comfortable home office with two work stations: one for Roth's photograph-studio business, the other dedicated to computer-based photographic work.

GARAGE BANDS

Garage-band musicians have the same industry-wide pride about the garage as computer companies do.

W here there are garages, there are garage bands. The same impulse that leads inventors and tinkerers to the backyard (privacy, seclusion, convenience) calls musicians—with the added bonus of a bit of distance between fledgling musicians and the house.

I'm not sure if there was an original garage band, but certainly Buddy Holly, who was all of 20 years old when his first hit "That'll Be the Day" topped the charts in 1958, practiced in a variety of garages in his hometown of Lubbock, Texas. His first band, formed with drummer Jerry Allison, was called Buddy and Bob; the Crickets came a couple of years later.

Even though "the day the music died" came far too soon, when Holly was only 22, the garage where Buddy Holly once practiced is still standing. In Holly's honor, Lubbock is home to the Buddy Holly Center (as well as the National Cowboy Symposium and the National Championship Chuckwagon Cookoff).

Nearly a half-century later, the garage band remains alive and well. In fact, garage-band musicians have the same industry-wide pride about the garage as computer companies do. Bands like Nirvana and Soul Asylum, as well as Creedence Clearwater Revival and the Kinks, all claim to have started out in someone's garage. Whether the garage itself inspires the so-called "garage-band sound" could be the subject of worthy speculation.

Self-proclaimed as "raw," garage bands run the gamut from the guitar-wailing of '60s psychedelic to bass and rhythm—dominated hip-hop to highly charged garage punk. The one exception to this might be Pat Metheny, whose jazzy guitar riffs can hardly be called "raw"—he dedicated a song and an album to the garage, both blessed with the catchy title "American Garage."

Although it's not much to look at, **this is where the subject of "the day the music died" was born: Buddy Holly and the Crickets got their start in this plain little garage back in the 1950s in Lubbock, Texas.**

All it takes: **a garage and a guitar.**

Straw-Bale Fruit Stand and Garage

THE ELLIS FARM IN UPSTATE NEW YORK has been in the family for three generations and was, until a decade ago, a dairy farm. Now planted with strawberries and raspberries, 30 acres of the farm are "U-pick" plants.

Norm and Connie Ellis and their three children dedicate summers to the berries. The rest of the year, Norm works as a general contractor. So when he decided to build a garage/fruit stand for the farm, he decided to try his hand at straw-bale construction, a building method in which straw bales are stacked to form the walls of the structure and then stuccoed over.

"I loved the thought of using common farm materials to build with," says Ellis. "And, of course, it occurred to me that perhaps this could blossom into a bale-building sideline, and that the garage could be a prototype of a small and comfortable home."

The upper level of the garage is accessible via an inner stairway. The lower floor is lined with shelves for displaying fruits and vegetables during the growing season. Ellis is contemplating leaving farming behind altogether, in which case the garage will become his workshop.

During the summer months, this garage, built of stuccoed-over straw bales, serves as a fruit stand for Ellis Fruit and Vegetables, a family farm in Upstate New York. The rest of the year, the garage returns to more garagelike functions—storing machinery and cars. Norm Ellis, who spends nongrowing-season months working as a general contractor, chose the straw-bale construction method because it uses a common farm material.

The three bays of the garage are open during the summer to display fruits and anything else they're trying to sell—like jam and canning supplies. Off-season, the garage functions as more of a farm shop—holding tractors and machinery, as well as a 1978 Datsun 280Z, which belongs to one of the Ellis's sons and is usually in a state of disrepair.

The cupola, which is not functional, does serve as a good place for a blue heron weather vane, in homage to the blue herons that return to the Upstate New York area. The hipped roof with a gable end reflects the house's roofline, as does the red border on the shingles. ✦

The garage sale is an American phenomenon.

The garage sale prevails **in neighborhoods across the country. Generating literally billions of dollars en masse, it's a venture that often begins in the garage and spills over into the driveway.**

THE GARAGE SALE

No venture is more suited for the garage than the sale. The garage sale is an American phenomenon: It happens in big cities and in small towns, mostly in warm weather, but in some parts of the country you'll find them year-round. According to those who know these sorts of things, in 1984 there were more garage sales than there were births, deaths, marriages, and divorces combined. The grand total of the take? Something close to $2 billion per year is transacted at all of those garage sales.

Americans started opening up their garage doors for sales at some point during the 1960s. Sociologists attribute the garage sale to postwar suburban affluence born in the 1950s. Decades later, regardless of economic condition, the garage sale prevails. Selling the "leftovers" from rearing children, the clothes that fit when we were younger, the outdated or replaced kitchen appliances, or the items we ourselves purchased at other garage sales is a hedge against clutter, an opportunity to make some extra cash, and an often futile response to the detritus of everyday life.

A Garage Library

The original barn/garage is being replaced with a " proper garage," designed in the spirit of Andrew Jackson Downing.

A LECTURER IN ART HISTORY at Williams College, Sheafe Satterthwaite also enjoys, in no particular order, the history of the American landscape, the designs of a Hudson River Valley gardener named Andrew Jackson Downing, and wrestling.

It might come as no surprise then that Satterthwaite's original barn/garage, in which all of the above activities took place, is being replaced, or rather added to, with a "proper garage," designed in the spirit of Andrew Jackson Downing. Downing, who wrote essays on architectural design and worked on the planning of the Mall in Washington, D.C., was a romantic at heart, who strived for balance, beauty, and naturalistic landscape design.

While the first garage was really a barn, with the hayloft converted into library office space and the tractor area transformed into a wrestling gymnasium, Satterthwaite feels that the new garage will be a vast improvement. For one, it will allow him to park his car.

A new garage, **which its owner refers to as "proper," is being added to the property. Designed as a timberframe structure, it reflects the symmetry and elegance of the work of Andrew Jackson Downing, an American landscape designer. The garage will feature a slate roof, as well as handcrafted garage doors with custom-made hardware.**

Inside, the library shows off the accumulation **of years of books, each reflecting the widespread interests of its owner. High ceilings, hardwood finishing, and a large window to the outside make it a perfect place for reflection and study.**

What the new garage brings is more living space for visiting family and friends, a woodshop, and three bays for cars and tractor equipment. Architect Merrall MacNeille looked to Downing's designs for the elegant form. Using two cubes that are 24 ft. by 48 ft. joined with a cross gable, MacNeille relied on symmetry for the ruling design principle. A sloped site gives the structure three stories at one level, and two for the main part of the garage. Three hinged doors lead to four parking bays: one is dedicated to a shop/woodworking area and includes a staircase that leads up to an apartment. Designed around a central living room, there are two guest bedrooms, as well as a bath and an office area. ✦

This barn/garage has been in service for many years to the intellectual pursuits of a professor, and includes a wrestling ring and some (albeit limited) off-street parking.

SETBACKS: WHERE THE GARAGE CAN GO

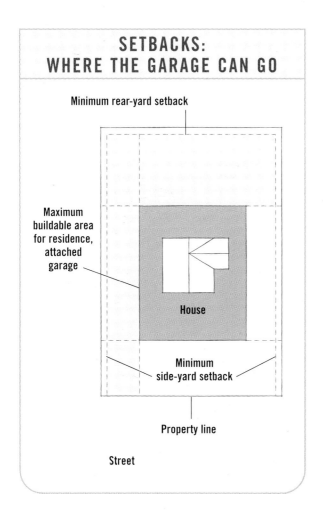

Minimum rear-yard setback

Maximum buildable area for residence, attached garage

House

Minimum side-yard setback

Property line

Street

A Variance Primer

A variance is essentially an authorization from the city or other jurisdiction for a property owner to vary a structure from an established set of zoning rules. These rules most often affect setbacks (how close to the property line you can build), height restrictions of garages, and in some instances, lot coverage (the ratio of permeable surfaces such as grass to hard-covered surfaces like driveways, patios, or the buildings themselves). If a proposed garage is too tall, too close to a property line, or simply too big, chances are that a variance will be needed.

The irony of variances is that although they usually don't ensure good design or aesthetic taste, they often inspire ingenuity and creativity. Yet the reality is that in some areas of the country a generic-kit garage will pass all zoning regulations, whereas a beautifully designed jewel box of a garage, which adds visually to the streetscape, will not pass if it happens to be 2 ft. too tall or is sited too close to a property line.

Garage *Leisure*

The owners of this former garage **are avid hobbyists, and the interior reflects their passions—from the watercolors to the antique terra cotta pots.**

THE GARAGE BECAME A PLACE for leisure just about the time that Americans started eating in the kitchen and gathering together for backyard barbecues. When American life became more informal, the typical American house tried first to adapt to the need for play space with the rec room.

The rec rooms I remember linger like a psychedelic dream—lava lamps, ping-pong tables, shag carpet. Most rec rooms were in garages or basements, since these were the only unclaimed places in the house. The garage rec room had all the advantages, however. Unlike the basement, the garage had windows and a big door that could open up and a floor that could be hosed down in the likely event of a spill.

The rec room has been replaced in most homes by the family room, which often can't accommodate much more than

A stone garage with a split personality: **garage in the winter and a potting shed when the weather warms up.**

What could be more American than the garage-mounted basketball hoop?

Anybody with $50 to spare can turn a garage and a driveway into a home basketball court.

a television and a home computer. One of the reasons new houses are getting bigger and bigger is that there seems to be no place in the typical floor plan for recreation. While the biggest houses—the "dream homes"—have rooms designated specifically for entertainment, billiards, and bridge, a garage designed to accommodate leisure activities can offer the best of all, with the additional advantage of flexible space that can be altered when the need arises.

The impulse to recreate in the garage cuts across many class barriers; witness the basketball hoop that adorns most garages. With a hoop screwed to the garage above the doors, the driveway becomes a court. Even the driveway can work for garage relaxation. In the summer or when the weather is mild, the driveway is an instant patio—a stretch of asphalt appropriate for everything from hopscotch to Super Bowl celebrations.

The garages in this chapter were designed and built with leisure in mind. They accommodate everything from plants to children; they offer places to swim, to picnic, and to play. ✦

The garage roof is planted with grass in the spring, part of the owner's ongoing commitment to the environment. Rather than use standard lap siding on the exterior, the owner chose plywood, which he stained by hand to give it a mottled appearance.

Bill West in his garage is a man at peace with the world—and with the careful organization of all his stuff. The author of *Your Garagenous Zone, the Complete Garage Organizer Guide,* West has developed a system of display boards and snap-together cabinetry to organize the typically unruly collection of garage tools and materials.

Grooved storage boards, originally designed to display retail merchandise, line the walls of the garage. A self-described garage organization expert, West finds that the storage system works much better than the old-fashioned pegboards.

Bill West's Garagenous Zone

BILL WEST SPENDS A LOT OF TIME thinking about garages. As a Colorado real estate agent, he's well versed in the advantages of attached and detached; as the author of *Your Garagenous Zone, the Complete Garage Organizer Guide,* he's become an expert in making the most of a space he calls the "home's final frontier."

"I've seen thousands of garages, and basically they're the same," West says. By that he means they're a mess—filled with clutter, badly conceived storage, and wasted space.

West's passion for garage organization began with a workbench. Dissatisfied with the typical 36-in.-high model, West experimented with building a bench that had a 42-in.-high countertop. The extra space made room to store a trash bin and a shop vac. He also found the usual workbench length unsatisfactory. His own bench occupies a whole wall of the garage—which still leaves him room for projects.

With clear organizing principles, among them "organize to visualize" (or if you see it, you can find it), West took on the chore of clearing out his own garage. Not only did he make it a finely tuned place for storage, he has also proved what he suspected—that the garage is the single best place for adding multipurpose space to the house.

The old pegboard is out, says West, who prefers to display tools on special grooved

panels that were created to display retail merchandise. West's garden tools hang there, as do whatever small tools he needs during a given project (otherwise, they're stored). West thinks that the retail display board, which sells at stores that cater to retailers for about $50 for a 4x8 sheet, is best for the simple reason that you don't have to keep putting nails in the wall. The organizational systems West used in his garage are plastic snap-together cabinets, available at any home-improvement store.

His passion for garage organization has become nothing short of gospel to "shift the attitude about the garage." West's garage is a bit of a temple—its organization lending itself to neighborhood tours and hosting any number of family events behind the garage doors. "We've done Sunday brunch, a New Year's party, a kid's birthday party, and a weekly 'Cigarage Night,'" says West. ✦

The garage is the single best place for adding multipurpose space to the house.

A Brief Guide to Garaganization

Bill West's garage guide is full of helpful recommendations both for using and for organizing the garage. Here are a few of his tips:

✦ De-clutter: Throw away or sell unwanted items.

✦ Organize to visualize: When you can see it, you can find it.

✦ Create a multipurpose room in the garage for family projects, fitness center, parties, hobbies, and crafts.

✦ Build a workbench that's 42 in. high. A tall work surface leaves room for trash or wet/dry vac storage below—and it's easier on your back.

✦ Install a swivel shelf on the garage wall for a television. That way you can work on projects and watch football at the same time.

✦ Put casters on the garage freezer and refrigerator to make cleaning easier.

✦ Paint garage floors with an industrial white epoxy finish. It will wear well, and white will make the space seem bigger.

✦ Maintain a stable temperature for comfort in colder months.

Bill West's garage **organization methods include a commercial wall storage system, bins, cabinets, drawers—and a television on a swivel stand mounted to the wall.**

Free-Time Carriage House

The garage that Jack Kachmarek built is dedicated to free time.

THE GARAGE THAT JACK KACHMAREK built is dedicated to free time. Located in a historic neighborhood, among several existing turn-of-the-20th-century carriage houses, this garage is in many ways a direct descendant of those big, multi-functional structures. It holds several cars on the first level, an interior basketball court, and upstairs a large expanse of space dedicated to billiards and parties.

The house the garage accompanies is from the Arts and Crafts era, a post-Victorian time that brought simpler, less ornate forms to architecture. Kachmarek wanted his new carriage house to match the main house: dormers, roofline, siding, windows, and doors are all related in some way to the house. Designed by Dennis Brose, of Period Design, the new garage blends well into its historic neighborhood.

The biggest design challenge was the site—long and narrow and parallel to the alley. The garage is sited so that Kachmarek can park his collection of

The garage, which appears to be bigger than the house, **is often mistaken for the main address. Designed to complement the 1912 house, the garage has been known to fool delivery people.**

The owner wanted his new garage to feel like a carriage house **to the main home, a circa 1912 Craftsman-style bungalow. The garage is designed to feature elements not found in most garages, such as the cupola and a colonnaded pergola-covered porch.**

cars either through garage doors that face the street or through hayloft doors that open onto the alley.

Inside, there are six parking spots, enough to park a small group of collectible cars, as well as Kachmarek's everyday vehicles. Glass-block windows were intended to echo horse-stall windows. Upstairs, about 1,000 sq. ft. of space is divided by a set of French doors topped by a leaded-glass transom. Kachmarek intends one area to eventually be a furniture-refinishing area; currently, it holds a rather stunning collection of Shriners' hats.

The rest of the square footage is what Kachmarek calls "a tribute to my misspent youth." This area showcases a 1912 Brunswick pool table and enough period smoke stands for a 1940s movie set; there's also a full bath. The entire upstairs is finished with wainscoting and a chair rail, in tribute to its Craftsman and carriage-house roots. ✦

The lower level of the garage **houses cars, six to be precise, with doors to the parking area letting onto the main street and the back alley. The ceiling is high enough for a game of basketball.**

The space upstairs is used for parties and billiards **and will eventually be used for furniture refinishing. Details like wainscoting and salvaged French doors were inexpensive ways to lend a sense of old-world elegance.**

The house is so distinctive that Nordgren felt that the garage needed to be just as unique.

Crowned with a gazebo, **this garage offers both a place to park and a place to picnic. A wooden fence, which alternates X's with parabolic curves, defines the picnic area—and keeps grandchildren from falling off.**

Crowned with a Gazebo

THERE ARE TWO GARAGES—three if you count the airplane hanger—on Loran Nordgren's Midwestern estate. Each has a different function: one holds the plane, one the tractor, and the third cars and picnics.

While consideration of function is certainly at work in the creation of any new house, Nordgren and architect Lou Heiser seemed determined also to have fun in this house, where color and whimsy are at play throughout. Nordgren was inspired by a trip to Scandinavia, where he toured the home of the artist Carl Larsson. Larsson (1853-1919) was a beloved painter in Sweden, who documented his family life on the walls of his own home with his characteristic lighthearted touch. It's this sense of whimsy and light that informs both Nordgren's house and garages.

What Nordgren identifies as the "regular garage" is crowned with an old-fashioned gazebo. Accessible by an exterior stairway that leads to the flat roof, the spot commands an impressive view of a small lake and rolling hills beyond. The garage is big enough for two cars and functions much as a garage should; the flat roof provides an outdoor sitting area

The Nordgren estate pays homage to the tradition of Swedish design; in particular, the owner was inspired by the work and home of 19th-century Swedish painter Carl Larsson. Designed by Lou Heiser, the house is spread across a rolling site, with various functions divided by different forms.

Traditionally, the **stabor** features a sod roof, kept clipped by grazing sheep or goats. This sod roof is planted with crocuses and daffodils and blooms in the early spring.

Built into the side of a small hill, **the garage for storing tractors pays homage to the Swedish** *stabor* **or storehouse. The exterior trim details and exposed timbers are traditional Swedish touches.**

with a view. The flooring is constructed from removable wood panels that can be taken up if roof repairs are needed. The hipped roof echoes the roofline of the house; the gazebo's whimsical fence helps give an outline to the structure and keeps small grandchildren from falling off.

Nordgren admits that it was actually the form of the house that inspired the gazebo. Sited on a slope of land, the house is so distinctive that Nordgren felt that the garage needed to be just as unique. As he puts it, "the size of the building demanded something taller from the garage building." Such attention to design resulted in a creative solution, which has made the garage among the most popular places in the house. ✦

You Can't Always Build What You Want

If your plans include a garage that's one-and-a-half or two stories tall, run your ideas by the local zoning department to see if the height of the garage you want to build meets local ordinances before going too far with the plans. Most cities establish height limits on buildings, depending on their use, location, and neighborhood character.

Each city is different, however, and the height a garage can be in a Minneapolis suburb can be far different from the height a garage can be in a historic Boston neighborhood. So while the house can be 35 ft. high, the accessory buildings, which include the garage, may be only 12 ft. high.

Most cities establish height limits on buildings, depending on their use, location, and neighborhood character.

Because detached accessory buildings can be built so close to lot lines, city officials usually like to keep them low so as not to shadow or stifle adjoining buildings. Another technicality is how the height is measured. Usually the height of a garage is not measured to the peak but to a point midway up the roof. A gable roof allows more light over it if it slopes away from the house, versus a

gable that faces the house and is always, therefore, a big wall blocking the light. Each situation is unique and each municipality has its say.

And there are many different reasons behind height restrictions. One reason may be aesthetic, so that in a neighborhood of one-story bungalows, the restrictions prevent somebody from building a two-story garage. Other reasons behind height limitations include keeping views open, maintaining the character of a neighborhood, and issues of scale.

Doug Haynes regularly hears **that the garage he designed for his Victorian home looks like it's always been there. While it's an enormous improvement to the neighborhood (replacing a condemned one-stall garage built in the 1940s), Haynes had to apply for a variance because of local height restrictions—and then fight neighborhood perceptions that the second level would become a rental unit.**

Garage Greenhouse

DOUG HAYNES AND DORIS FORTINO built their garage as a result of the confluence of three things: a collection of old leaded windows discovered in an antique store, the need for a flexible space outside the house, and a pressing need for a place to put the car.

The existing one-stall garage was on the verge of being condemned; it remained standing only because a previous owner had reinforced its walls by nailing on sheets of plywood. Haynes, a graphic designer, first decided that their new garage would be stylistically more appropriate to their Victorian home. His design incorporated similar elements from the house—steep roofline, the columns, and the mix of clapboards and shingle siding. And then there were the windows, which would make the garage, at least in part, a greenhouse.

"We considered carefully the idea of building a structure that would be multifunctional. It seemed like an enormously practical undertaking—to make the most of the structure, both visually and in terms of its function."

The garage that Haynes and Fortino built offers space for three or four cars: two in the garage, a third in the carport space, and a fourth, if necessary, in the greenhouse. When a

The brick pavers **that surround the garage were all salvaged from city repaving projects. They extend around the greenhouse and become a backyard patio.**

car's not in it, the greenhouse becomes a backyard destination. The area above the garage was designed to be big enough to convert into either a studio or a gym. Right now it serves as Doug's workshop.

With its front porch doubling as a carport, the space above the garage is ready to become anything from an extra bedroom to an office. And with the greenhouse opening onto a formal garden, this garage is an example of a structure that makes the most of its function. ◆

This garage is an example of a structure that makes the most of its function.

New Life for Old Windows

The appeal of old windows, particularly if they're beautiful (or were a good deal), is universal. In garages, the window is perhaps the most used recycled or reclaimed item. Windows are necessary in garages—they bring in light and air and let out harmful fumes. And while they also can have great character and tell stories of the past, they can look out of place if improperly used.

For instance, windows that swing open (called casement windows) or true divided-lite windows (with individual panes or lites of glass, rather than one big pane overlaid with a vinyl grid) give the garage an older feel, while windows with a cross-hatch pattern of lites can lend a Tudor style. And, there are compelling aesthetic reasons to give the garage the same style as the house:

a Tudor garage for a 1950s rambler might not be the ticket.

Often, the style of the found materials can inspire the design of the building. The garage greenhouse featured here came to be built because its owners found a set of old, leaded casement windows at an antique store. This garage sits near a Victorian house, and the old-fashioned feel of the garage blends well with the existing architecture. Yet there are challenges in re-use: Older windows are not always the most energy efficient, they may need refurbishing, and there's often a limited quantity of a particular type. And with any reused building material, you have to bring it back to the original state, which can involve scraping away 40 years worth of paint.

The windows, **which came from a mansion in the area, were bought years before the garage was built and put away to await just the right use. They eventually inspired the owners to build a garage that could also be a greenhouse.**

The steep roof pitch on one side is expanded by a dormer entry into the second level. The stairs are on the exterior, to save interior square footage, and lead up the side of the building to a small landing in the treetops.

Jazz Room

THIS HOMEOWNER WENT THROUGH the usual considerations when building his garage. Step one: Think about the budget. Step two: Wonder why the garage, at half the size of the house and built almost identically, does no more than hold the car? Step three: Think about making something more out of the space.

Which is how this garage came to be called, early in the planning process, "the jazz room." The owner loves to listen to jazz, but the size of the smallish family house meant that everyone else had to listen as well. Architects Mark Osburn and Wayne Clarke designed the garage to hold two cars, and connected it to the house at ground level.

Upstairs, the designers made the most of the room by placing the stairs outside, therefore not eating up valuable interior space, an option that works well in this mild climate. The railing bumps out on one side to make room for a bench.

The architects opted to leave the framing exposed; whitewashed, it makes the jazz room feel like a weekend retreat. French doors off the living room lead to a balcony, which further extends the space. Two beds are tucked into an alcove created by the asymmetrical roofline so the jazz room does double duty as a guest room. ◆

A SIMPLE LIVING ARRANGEMENT

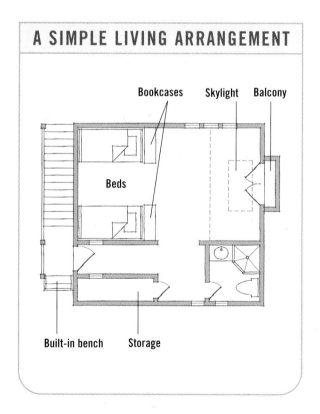

Bookcases Skylight Balcony

Beds

Built-in bench Storage

The garage jazz room is big enough for a couch and chair, and with beds tucked into alcoves (not shown) it doubles as a guest room. The exterior stairway and the second-floor entrance are sheltered by a gable dormer. On the gable end facing the house, a small French balcony expands the interior space outside.

This garage addition to a Dutch Colonial home is dedicated to the children in the family. Because the garage addition is the first thing a visitor sees, the architect took care to make it look like it was part of the house. The existing garage was transformed into storage space and a connecting mudroom.

A Garage for Kids

THE PLAYFUL KIDS' SPACE that architect Richard Kawalek designed for a young family in northeastern Ohio began with the simple need for more room. The growth of their family had left the couple with a much-loved house that just wasn't big enough; two of the kids shared a bedroom, and there was little or no space to play, except in the basement.

The siting of the house, on a cliff with views of a valley, made it virtually impossible to expand. The attached garage seemed the best option, but its placement on the front of the house meant that the new garage would be the first thing a visitor saw. The new and improved garage that Kawalek designed had to become an attractive part of the house.

Taking visual cues from the family's Dutch Colonial home, Kawalek designed the garage with a barn-line gambrel roof, lots of windows, and a cupola. The existing garage was essentially subsumed by the renovation and addition, becoming a mudroom and storage area connecting the parking spaces with the first

The children's room combines bedroom function with play space. The loft in the middle is constructed from gnarly logs and rises to the peak of a 16-ft. ceiling. The architect used various techniques to create smaller spaces within the larger space, such as a loft, small private window seats, niches, and nooks—all scaled to the size of kids.

The gambrel roof dormer, window boxes, small windows on the first level, and other architectural details all combine to help the garage look like part of the house.

Design Challenges and Solutions

The challenges

- ✦ Create more space in a house with little room to expand
- ✦ Maintain design integrity of existing house
- ✦ Make room for cars
- ✦ Create a space for kids to live and play

The solutions

- ✦ Build out and over existing garage
- ✦ Add gambrel roof, many windows, and cupola to echo main house
- ✦ Turn old garage into mudroom/laundry and put cars in first-floor addition
- ✦ Create large kids' area with full bath over existing garage

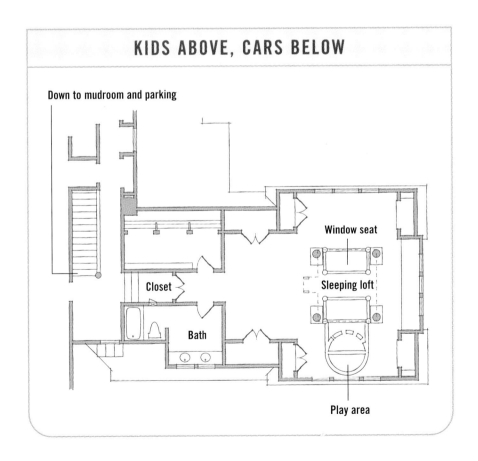

KIDS ABOVE, CARS BELOW

Down to mudroom and parking

Window seat

Closet

Sleeping loft

Bath

Play area

A kids' bathroom was a necessary part of the renovation. Located off the hallway that connects the new space to the house, the bathroom occupies a dormer in the old garage. The owners are enamored with the Western motif, which is clearly evident in the bathroom, with its horseshoe light fixture. The sinks have each child's name impressed into the galvanized metal surround.

Four window seats, one on each side of the room, offer space for homework and lots of play. By adding pillows on top of the window seats, the owners created sleepover space.

level of the house. The new space above the garage joins the new kids' quarters to the house.

Upstairs, big windows, rough-cut beams, and a pine floor make the space light and airy. With its 16-ft. ceilings, the interior accommodates a mini-basketball court and a freestanding bedroom/loft platform made from gnarly logs. The alcoves in the corners are for sleeping; the window seats double as beds for sleepovers. ✦

UP ON THE ROOF

With the right planning, the garage can bring outdoor living space to the house. And sometimes a space that works only seasonally can be just the sort of place you want. If you're considering adding an attached garage, consider a flat roof for it. A peaked roof will block views from the house. An attached garage, with a flat roof and the proper egress and support system, can become a deck, a kid's play space, or, with even more planning and structural support, a place to put a swimming pool.

If the garage roof deck is going to be private, access to it should be from the house, maybe off the master bedroom. If it's a more public space, it makes sense to access the deck via an exterior stair.

An attached garage with a flat roof can become a deck.

Glulam beams **crossed by heavy-duty wood I-joists form the structure that supports this 20,000-lb. lap pool and hot tub on the roof of a garage in Seattle, Washington.**

The flat roof on this home's garage **matches the flat-roof, contemporary style of the home. Yet a flat roof topped by a deck can be added to any type of home with the proper structural support and waterproofing.**

Pool-House Parking

THE CLIENTS NEEDED A GARAGE, a pool house, and an art studio. The outbuilding that New York architect Frederic Schwartz designed meets all three requirements.

It was actually local zoning regulations (fairly restrictive in this historic neighborhood) that inspired the combination structure. The zoning rules were designed to prohibit the use of a second residence on the same property as the primary residence—so it couldn't be rented or sold. Although local laws would allow up to three structures on the property, none could have full services unless connected with breezeways. Schwartz thought the breezeway idea felt inappropriate for the northern climate, so instead he designed one building to serve all functions.

The neoclassical, shingled garage that Schwartz designed is intended to "be in conversation with the house," as he puts it. The architect kept the scale of the pool house relatively small—26 ft. by 20 ft., which is standard for a two-car garage. He used every square foot to maximum advantage. The first level is taken up by garage space, a narrow cabana area for changing clothes, and a front porch accented by neoclassical columns and stairs that face the pool. The second level is divided into two areas, both in use as art studios.

Recognizing that the most important aspect in secondary buildings is their adaptability, Schwartz ingeniously designed for change.

The pool side of the building features a deep porch and a shingled roof that's supported by three columns, all of which were inspired by architect Gunnar Asplund's Woodland Chapel in Stockholm. The stairs in front literally elevate this small building: It's an architectural statement that insists upon the significance of a small outbuilding.

Everything inside the garage was considered for possible conversion into something else. The pool cabana at the back of the garage (facing the pool) could be turned into a kitchen, because it was plumbed during construction. The art studio could be converted into two bedrooms connected by a bath. ✦

The architect wanted both house and garage structures to work together stylistically: Entrances share neoclassical design elements—most evident, a column that serves to define both buildings. The garage doors are set back, which helps disguise the parking function of the building.

The Hangout

This garage was built in conjunction with a new house: both were designed with a tight budget in mind and make the most of simple forms. The garage is essentially a box, but a tin roof, a well-placed light and wall planter, and a stunning garage door all enliven what could have been nothing more than basic. The extension of the roofline brings storage facilities to a garage that was intended to be a getaway: the owners store a lawn mower, ladders, and a kayak under the roof.

THE HOUSE AND GARAGE that architect Ross Chapin designed for a newly married couple in their 40s has two living rooms: one in the house, where they entertain, the other in the garage (considered "hangout space"), where their hobbies and interests find expression.

The garage, as Chapin explains, was never intended to hold cars; rather, the couple wanted a place to work on their collection of bicycles, to exercise, and to listen to music and read. The reason it looks like a garage is that should they ever want to sell, the parking function could be easily restored.

One thing the clients wanted was a light-filled workspace. The garage door, with its big glass panels, floods the space with light and was well worth the money: $400 more than the cost of a regular paneled door. Windows on both the south and west walls bring in consistent light during the day; the glass garage door on the east side brings in morning light. The interior is finished roughly for a reason: The clients didn't want the space to feel like the house.

Chapin placed the garage about 50 ft. from the house, understanding that the walk offers a mental transition from garage to house. The garage is about 18 ft. by 24 ft., or in parking terms, one-and-a-half stalls. With details similar to the house, the garage was considered a priority and yet used up only 15 percent of the entire $100,000 budget for the house. ✦

The garage was never intended to hold cars; rather, the couple wanted a place to work on their collection of bicycles, to exercise, and to listen to music and read.

Inside, the garage continues the space of the house. It's the place where the owners do everything but park: a workshop for bicycles, a couch, refrigerator, and stereo system provide excellent hangout space. The garage also brings informal space to a small house: At just over 1,000 sq. ft., the house contains everything it should, and the garage is essentially an extension of the living quarters.

Living in the Garage

THE OFFICIAL TERM FOR GARAGE LIVING is "accessory
dwelling unit," a description that works only in the most
perfunctory way to describe the great variety of garages that
offer everything from extra income to peace of mind.

I've always thought of the accessory dwelling unit as the
mother-in-law apartment, but its usefulness extends beyond
that concept. Garage living has been immortalized in such TV
classics as *My Favorite Martian* (in which an ad man allows a
stranded Martian to hide out in his garage) and *Happy Days*
(in which The Fonz lived atop the Cunninghams' garage).
Such garage quarters, with separate entrance, bath, and
kitchen, can offer the perfect insurance policy for guests who
stay longer than three days.

Of all garages being built today, nearly 20 percent include
garage livable space. Sometimes the garage *is* the dwelling
unit; built before the house, these "starter garages" offer a

This cedar-shingled garage **features custom
garage doors made from red cedar, reinforced at each
joint with copper plates. A boardwalk connects the
garage to the house.**

Starter garages combine the best of apartment life with home ownership, and they come with a parking space.

 could not have been called *Happy Days* if The Fonz had moved into the Cunninghams' spare bedroom. Better for everyone that he lived in an apartment above their garage.

place to live and to park. The advantages of building the house before the garage may seem obvious: a place to cook versus a place to park; a place to bathe versus a place to park. But consider a garage with live-in potential, one that combines the efficiency of apartment living with its own parking spot; a garage waiting to become—once the house is built—a guest suite, a home office, or a rental.

Lots of people today are building their garages before they build the house. These starter garages combine the best of apartment life with home ownership, and they come with a parking space. In the newfound appreciation for smaller living spaces, this kind of arrangement gets high points for simplicity and efficiency. The starter garages featured in this chapter range from a budget starter model to a high-end garage home.

Whether fancy or plain, the fundamental principle of design remains the same—efficient use of a small space. And as finances improve, the owners move on, usually into the accompanying house on the same property. And if you play out this scenario, the starter garage becomes the mother-in-law apartment.

Every garage has potential for living space. With the proper design and planning it can bring adaptable, useful space to any home. This chapter features garages with full-scale quarters on top; garages with master bedrooms; garages that have been transformed into full-time cottages. And there are garages that simply function as getaways, proving the maxim that even the happiest of families needs a livable garage. ◆

Small Wonders

This garage, of mid-1930s vintage, contained an attic-type space that the owners wanted to turn into an apartment that could serve as a hangout for a teenage daughter.

THERE'S NOT AN INCH OF WASTED SPACE in this 350-sq.-ft. garage apartment, which builder Robert Malone designed for a California couple with a teenage daughter. The small size of this one-car garage created an immediate challenge: to add apartment facilities that would ensure that the space could function as a guest suite when the daughter left home for college.

The 1930s-era garage had a steep pitch to its roof but not nearly enough buildable space to include anything more than a cot. By adding three dormers, Malone gained enough space to create a surprisingly spacious apartment that miraculously manages to feature a fireplace.

The first challenge proved to be in the garage's foundation, which wasn't hefty enough to hold the weight of a second floor. To remedy the deficiency Malone poured new concrete footings under the existing foundation. The foundation was further strengthened with the

A small window dormer creates an alcove inside, just big enough for the bed. No space is overlooked: A desk fits into a corner; storage is built in to the kneewalls. Roof windows bring light and views in through the sloped ceiling. Every possible spot is lined with shelves or places for storage, essential in a small space.

Builder Robert Malone considers attic remodels a favorite project. With 350 sq. ft. to work with, Malone knew that dormers would be a great way to create interior alcoves and nooks. By adding the small gable streetside, as well as two larger shed dormers, Malone was able to create a plan that offers a sitting area, bed alcove, kitchenette, and fireplace.

addition of a grid of steel reinforcement connected to steel pins set into the original foundation.

The existing attic floor was framed with 2x4s, as most garages are, which meant that the structure had to be beefed up to support the weight of a living space above. While most wall framing is built from 2x6 studs, that standard construction would have added 2 in. to each wall, and in such a small space would have reduced the square footage by 30 sq. ft., a significant loss of precious space. The mild California climate allowed him to frame with the minimal 2x4s, because insulation needs were minor.

Planning for the mechanical requirements was also informed by the need to avoid eating up valuable living space. This garage, which was not originally attached to the house, was connected through an existing linen closet on the home's second floor. The mechanical chase went between the new garage's bathroom and a bathroom on the house's second floor.

The key to fitting bathroom, bedroom, kitchen, storage, and living space into 350 sq. ft., according to Malone, was careful planning and small-scale appliances. Using one essentially open space, Malone created separate areas within it for kitchen and bath in alcoves, which help differentiate the space. Built-in shelves and closets above the eaves allow for a place to hide clutter, essential in small-space living. ✦

There's not an inch of wasted space in this 350-sq.-ft. garage apartment.

The bathroom is a study in efficiency.
The toilet is rear-discharge, which solved some planning problems; the laundry hamper is in the wall, with a towel bar as its handle.

Design Challenges and Solutions

The challenges
✦ Create a fully equipped apartment in a 350-sq.-ft. garage
✦ Build in sufficient upstairs space
✦ Strengthen foundations and attic floor
✦ Find place for heating/AC system

The solutions
✦ Carefully plan an open space to include multiple functions
✦ Add three dormers to the steep roof for headroom
✦ Pour new footings and tie to existing foundation
✦ Run ductwork to garage through bathroom in home

Built in 1994 for under $50,000, **this carefully planned starter garage offers enough space for a young couple and a fledgling contracting business.**

Simple Starter on a Small Budget

MOST OF US KNOW that the things we want from a home—a place to eat, sleep, bathe, and relax—are all achievable on a small scale. This contractor started by designing a small three-bedroom house, envisioned as a "starter home" for himself and his fiancée.

However, on the brink of marriage and starting up a new contracting business, he knew that whatever he built would need to be a place he could grow into. It was the need for a place to keep his tools and a truck that inspired the idea of first building a garage with an upstairs loft—a place comfortable for two adults in the beginning of their relationship that would grow and change as they did.

Its 24-ft. by 30-ft. size, big enough for two garage stalls, provided room for the contracting business on the first level and 720 sq. ft. of living space upstairs. The stairs were built outside to save square footage and to keep the interior plan open, which makes it feel bigger. Because the living space was to be occupied by a couple, the only necessary area of privacy was the bathroom. To keep the space light and

Stairs, Inside and Out

Interior stairs can eat up lots of space both upstairs and down. In the case of a two-car, 250-sq.-ft. garage, the stairway takes up at least 50 sq. ft., so thought should be given to where it's placed.

If you live in a cold climate, or if the space upstairs is used by the same people who park in the lower level, it makes sense to place the stairs inside. An interior stairway shouldn't go directly in the parking area; separating the entry and parking functions creates more of a sense of entry. A small entranceway or foyer, which is accessible through a door in the parking area, creates a transition area, not unlike the mudroom that connects the garage to a same level.

Exterior stairs allow you to use the full interior space. They are particularly a good idea in warmer climates and when the upper level is rented to someone other than the owner.

Understanding that interior stairs can eat up valuable square footage in such a small home, the owner built exterior stairs to lead up to the loft.

The living space benefits from windows on all four sides. **Two dormers create an alcove for the bed and a window seat, which opens for storage. Even the bed hides drawers underneath.**

airy, the bathroom has a curtained glass door, which allows light to stream through.

Everything is planned to fit

The living space is open to the bedroom, which is essentially a bed built into an alcove; the kitchen is part of the living area, separated by a country table; a window seat offers another place to sit. Carefully designed storage was essential to keep this small space livable, so storage is built into every conceivable nook and cranny. The bed has drawers underneath and the kneewall space next to the bed has been transformed into two large clothes closets. The window seat opens to function as a chest. And the kneewalls at the eaves feature short doors that lead to additional storage right under the roof.

Varied ceiling heights throughout modulate the space and help create a sense of different areas within the larger space. The living and dining areas benefit from the cathedral pitch of the roof, while 8-ft. ceilings make the bedroom, the bathroom, and the window-seat area feel a little cozier. A woodstove in the living area becomes a hearth for the home and its main heat source.

This starter garage will work for the couple for as long as their lives maintain this status quo. With the addition of a child or the expansion of the business, the starter garage can become an office, a rental, or even a full-fledged house with the addition of extra bedrooms. ✦

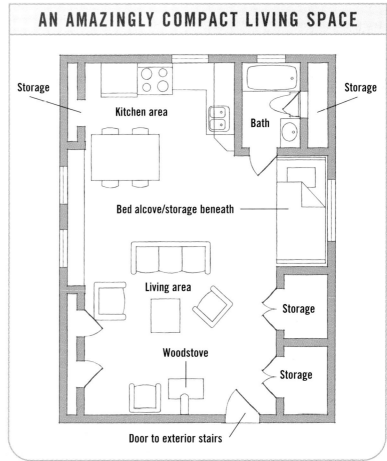

AN AMAZINGLY COMPACT LIVING SPACE

Storage

Kitchen area

Storage

Bath

Bed alcove/storage beneath

Living area

Storage

Woodstove

Storage

Door to exterior stairs

The parking side of the carriage house is sided with clapboards, while the rest of it is shingled. While the owners live in the lot behind, they use the carriage house to park and rent out the upstairs apartment. The driveway is poured concrete, which is colored and patterned to resemble pavers.

Rhode Island Rental

WHAT WAS ONCE A GARAGE has been replaced by a carriage house, which befits a historic neighborhood in Rhode Island. City zoning laws were so restrictive that the owners enlisted architects Maria Aureli and Charles Ficke to design a full-story house, which could also hold the cars.

Designed with the same details as the house, this carriage house is a full two stories, offering parking and a workshop on the ground level and a full-size second-story apartment above. The house has two entrances, one through garage doors, the other through elegant double doors, which lead to a 6-ft. by 7-ft. heated space, a sort of combination mudroom and foyer that opens both to the stairs and to the garage.

The second-level apartment benefits from the gambrel roofline. The varied ceiling height gives proportion to areas of the living space—which is essentially open: kitchen, dining, and living areas flow together, while French doors lead into the bedroom area. The pattern in the wood floor emphasizes the length of the space and lends a touch of elegance. ✦

The apartment upstairs is a full story, and the line of the gambrel roof influences the ceiling, giving a relatively simple interior some interesting variation. A nook, created by the roofline, makes room on the inside for a couch.

The gambrel roofline of this Newport, Rhode Island, carriage house matches the Dutch Colonial house, but the structure is very much its own building. Elegant French doors connect the house to the backyard. The entrance leads through a heated space to the parking-area stairs to the upper level.

Living in the Roof

Most living arrangements in a garage are of the second-story variety. Because most detached garages are one-and-a-half stories at most (there are height restrictions on outbuildings), the second story has the same amount of floor area as the main level but often less headroom. However, the shape, pitch, and angles of the roof can be a design advantage. It's the slope of the roof, the location of windows, and the coziness of dormers that create a living space unlike any other; filled with a variety of volumes and angles, it expresses shelter in a fundamental way. Perhaps because the roof is so near, the feeling of being sheltered from the elements seems more immediate.

While this garage appears to have two parking bays, it really has three, though the third was added for storage space. The door on the gable end leads to the storage bay and to the stairs.

Overflow Garage

IT HAD BEEN MORE THAN a decade since Dr. Kevin Zorski worked as a builder. But the purchase of oceanfront property in Maine inspired him to build again, starting with the garage. "I wanted to try a couple of things out before we built our house," he says and enumerates the challenges he wanted to take on: "exposed rafters, handmade windows, and stonework."

With help from various contractors, the garage he built features all those things, and it stakes out the area where Zorski and family hope to put a house a few years down the road. With a 22-ft. by 32-ft. footprint, the garage is designed to hold two cars, with an extra bay added for storage (the heavy clay soil on the property prohibited a basement in the house).

Laying the stones

Zorski's interest in working with stone inspired the hand-laid foundation, constructed from stones salvaged from a local sandpit. The windows, another design challenge, proved less satisfactory. Zorski wanted casement windows that opened in, which he figured would be easier to clean. The effort of transforming barn sash into casement windows was, in the end, not worth the hard work, he thinks.

This garage apartment is about 700 sq. ft. and uses every possible inch—as a guest room, home office, playroom, and place to entertain. When the house it accompanies is completed, the garage will become a guest house. The area behind the woodstove has been plumbed for eventual use as a kitchen.

Eventually, the house will be erected about 10 ft. from the garage and will be finished with the same cedar shingles, dormers, and stone foundation.

The garage has doors on two sides: One leads into the storage bay, the other into the parking area. The garage has become a secondary living space:

 an everyday office for his wife, who works as a commodities trader, as well as a place to entertain guests who visit their temporary, cramped mobile home. A bedroom and bath allow the garage to function as a guest room, while their young son has claimed a small area in the kneewall of the upstairs bedroom for LEGO bricks. While there's no kitchen, the front bay is plumbed for that eventual addition.

The interior is finished with an eye on the budget, but careful use of natural materials gives the space elegance. The floor and walls are inexpensive pine. The same salvaged slate used on the roof was cut into 5-in. by 5-in. tiles for the bathroom floor.

Eventually, the house will be erected about 10 ft. from the garage and will be finished with the same cedar shingles, dormers, and stone foundation. In the meantime, the garage is what its builder considers "a sanity-keeping device." ✦

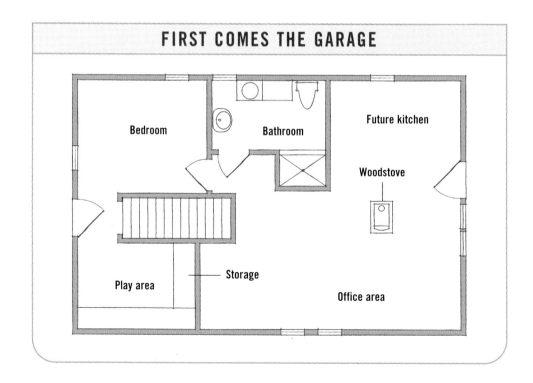

FIRST COMES THE GARAGE

Bedroom

Bathroom

Future kitchen

Woodstove

Storage

Play area

Office area

A New England Assemblage

From the street, the garage doesn't look like a garage.

WHEN RALPH AND VALERIE VITALE's home was built in 1726, it didn't come with a garage. Over the centuries, various owners had made their mark on the house, modernizing and expanding it to connect with an existing barn on the property. But in all its variations, the house never had a place to park the cars.

When it came time to add a three-car garage, Ralph and Valerie determined that it could also function as guest quarters, removed from family living areas but connected to the house. They wanted to be sensitive to their historic home and to the neighborhood, which has a very active historic-district commission that must approve all renovations.

The immediate challenge for architect Benjamin Nutter was to design a structure that would not present a monolithic garage-door face to the street. Because the addition would be joining a series of additions, Nutter determined to use as inspiration the tradition of New England assembled houses that appear to be collections of connected structures.

From the street, the garage doesn't look like a garage, an essential condition to getting the building approved by the historic commission. Windows on the

Architect Benjamin Nutter's garage addition echoes the traditional low-slung assembled buildings of New England. Reading the building from left to right: the original circa 1726 house; an addition that connects the house with an old barn on the property, now in service as a library and home office; a connecting mudroom and separate entrance; the garage addition.

Nutter used a "broken roof" to minimize the size of the garage addition. It was integrated into the garden by placing the garage doors on the side and making the garage look as houselike as possible. A window seat (in the large shed dormer) has great views of a perennial garden.

first level continue the window pattern of the house; the garage door faces away from the street.

On the second level, the new garage adds two new bedrooms and a full bath to the house. The historic look of the original even carries over inside the addition, using the same molding, flooring, and an old door salvaged from the house. A walkway connects the second floor of the house to the apartment above the garage. ✦

The garage addition has its own entrance, **essential for other possible future uses of the space. While the owners use it for a home office and for overnight guests, a future owner might find the garage suite useful for a live-in au pair or for elderly parents. This entrance is also a mudroom for the family and a way to the house. The stairway leads up to a second-level catwalk that connects the addition with a loft space in the adjoining barn.**

New Garages for Historic Homes

The design of a garage for a historic home, especially if the home is on the historic register or in a historic district, involves presenting plans to a commission that looks specifically at the appropriateness of the design.

Architect Joe Metzler, a member of the Minneapolis Heritage Preservation Commission, says that a mistake most people make is assuming their garage will be historically accurate if they merely add the same decorative details to it that are found on the house. Good detailing is important, but it should always be part of a good design.

Metzler recommends that the design of a garage for a historic house should be carefully thought out to consider:

◆ roof pitch and overhang

◆ window styles

◆ exterior materials

◆ stylistic detailing unique to the house

Also, the scale and position of the garage should be appropriate to the house. One way to think about a new garage for a historic home: It should look as if it has always been there.

The hallway upstairs **leads directly into the bedroom areas. The pine-plank flooring and molding, consistent with the rest of the house, makes the garage addition feel more like a continuation of the home, rather than something separate.**

Carefully designed to match **the 1912 Craftsman house, this garage replaced a 1940s garage that did nothing more than hold one car. The design achieves its elegance through simplicity and carefully considered details.**

Designer Tom Holleman **designed and made this ceramic medallion of St. George battling the dragon, which Holleman sees as a parable of good triumphing over evil. Besides, says the designer, "it's an excuse to draw a great horse."**

Handmade Haven

THE GARAGE THAT TOM HOLLEMAN designed and built for his friends, Jeff and Melissa Gembis, is a jewel of a structure.

Holleman "retired" from a job with a large architectural firm more than 15 years ago. He had become frustrated with the process: "It was too hectic; the projects were too spread out. While I worked on countless designs or schemes, I never got to see them built." Holleman has been working in what he calls "the fun way" for the past 15 years with partner and carpenter Eric Vogel. The two take on only one or two projects a year—"we've reconciled ourselves that we aren't going to get rich, but we get a good night's sleep, and everyone we work for remains our friends," he explains.

Special details to complement the house

The Craftsman-inspired garage came after Holleman and Vogel had completed an extensive remodeling for the Gembis's house. Using the same materials—cedar shakes and brick—Holleman designed a garage with a historic feel that looks more in keeping with the 1912 house than the previous 1940s model did.

Holleman takes care to imbue all of his projects with special details. Doors are custom-

The interior is finished simply, **and indestructibly, with beadboard, a material the architect discovered to be virtually child resistant. Adults and kids alternate the use of the space—although it's essentially a playroom for both. There's abundant storage in the eaves, in closets, and in kneewall space.**

Another ceramic detail enlivens the space between windows in the garage dormer: a mosaic crowing rooster, which signals the break of day.

built of oak. "People take for granted walking through a door, but a beautiful entranceway gives the people who enter delight," he says. There are two ceramic medallions, which Holleman designed himself. One, on the garage's front, is a rooster signaling the break of day. The other, an inset ceramic medallion of St. George, faces the backyard.

Although local zoning laws prohibited the addition of a full-scale apartment, it made sense to both designer and client that the garage include enough space so it could be used as a getaway from the house. The couple has three small children, so Holleman finished the area on top of the garage to double as an escape. The beadboard gives it an elegance suitable for entertaining friends, while it has also proved to be resistant to both tricycles and in-line skates. ✦

MAKING THE MOST OF THE ENTRANCE

The most used entrance to the house is usually through the garage or in the door that is closest to where we park. And yet, both entrances—to the garage and to the house—are often overlooked in terms of design and planning.

A Pattern Language (Christopher Alexander et al., Oxford University Press, 1977), a book that's become the bible for designers and urban planners, suggests that it's imperative to "make something of the space that connects the house and the car, to make it a positive space—a space that supports the experience of coming and going."

Entrances create a sense of welcome. If the garage is attached, consider the connection between garage and house so that people don't enter past piles of recycling and the cat's litter box. *A Pattern Language* goes so far as to suggest that the garage be connected to the main entrance of the house so that the main entrance is used every day.

If the garage is detached from the house, make the most of the transition space between the two structures. And the garage's entrance can be as beautiful as any entrance to the house. In the garage entrance shown here, the architect planned for a small, covered foyer that boasts a custom-built door, beautifully crafted hardware, and an arched entranceway.

"People take for granted walking through a door, but a beautiful entranceway gives the people who enter delight."

This entrance was designed **to create a feeling of delight for those who use it. The door was custom-made by the architect and his partner; the wrought-iron hardware was handmade in France; the arched beams echo a shape on the home's porch.**

Garage Beautiful

The interior is finished **with high-end materials such as knot-free roof trusses, tiled fireplace surround, and custom cabinetry. The open floor plan maximizes the spaciousness of the apartment.**

BACK DURING THE 1980s, Haverson Architecture and Design designed a house in Westchester County, New York, for a couple of young professionals who wanted space and elegance. Ten years later, the architect who designed the house encountered its new owners at a zoning and planning commission meeting. They were applying for a variance to put living quarters in the garage.

Jay Haverson introduced himself and soon found himself designing the renovation to his original design. What the new owners envisioned was a small, elegant apartment over the garage for the wife's mother.

Zoning laws limited the garage renovation to its original size; therefore, the original 880 sq. ft. of garage became

Both garage and house, **with their gingerbread trim and multiple gables, evoke the Victorian era, yet the house is new and was designed for a young professional family. The garage was renovated 10 years earlier, and then again by the same architects for different clients to transform it into a small house for visiting family.**

880 sq. ft. of garage apartment. The architect convinced his clients to spend their money on quality of space, creating in effect a small house in which all spaces are in use every day.

Three gables mark the front and echo the gables on the house's exterior: two bays are for parking, the third is dedicated to the entrance, which leads to the stairs. For the design of the interior, the architects listened to the person who would live there, a sophisticated woman in her late 60s, who wanted a comfortable, personable space where she could entertain friends but also be part of her daughter's family.

Inside, dining, living, and kitchen functions blend easily in an open, airy space. The bedroom, which occupies about a third of the upstairs, is private and luxurious. There is plenty of well-thought-out storage—offered in large closets, a pantry, linen closet, and television nook.

High-quality finishing details, such as cedar ceiling beams, hardwood floors, and a kitchen finished in cherry, make the public areas feel warm and welcoming. The garage is, in fact, still the garage for the house, but so complete was the renovation the owners now refer to it as the "cottage." ✦

Three gables mark the front and echo the gables on the house's exterior.

The bedroom has a view of the treetops and the house. So convincing is this garage's transformation, that even though the owners still use the lower level as a garage, they now refer to the structure as the "cottage."

Three bay spaces, one dedicated to the entrance, mark the garage and help tie it visually to the house. The scale, which is quite wide, is minimized by the columns, the symmetrical quality, and the central bay with its walkout balcony.

A Fire Station Echo

For more than 200 years, Great Diamond Island has been a destination for artists and writers. Accounts tell of visits by such luminaries as poet Henry Wadsworth Longfellow and writer Harriet Beecher Stowe, as well as a steady stream of painters enraptured by the dramatic landscape off the coast of Maine. The clientele changed radically by the turn of the last century, when the U. S. Army designed and built Fort McKinley there to defend the harbor during the Spanish-American War.

The barracks and buildings were built in the Queen Anne style and were used by the military until 1945. Over the next 50 years, the site turned into a sort of ghost town, with the brick buildings still standing but the life of the place gone. Eventually, the remains of the army buildings were purchased by a developer with the idea that the compound could be renovated into high-end housing. With all structures on the National Register of Historic Places, it was essential that the renovations preserve the architectural integrity of the site.

When the owners first acquired the firehouse, it was just a sturdy shell on a granite foundation. Architect Peter Edwards respected the building's original function in his renovation of the structure into an elegant, compact weekend home. The two bays for fire engines were kept and the front wall recessed to create a porch. The hose-drying tower, now shingled with slate, is a cupola-sized room, accessible by a ladder.

An ingenious renovation

A businessman and his family hired architect Peter Edwards to renovate the old firehouse, a structure that originally held the horse-drawn fire carriages for the island. The structure was nothing more than a shell, but Edwards was determined to keep the essence of the building by preserving the outlines of its original firehouse function.

The interior features simple materials, like wood wainscoting and pine flooring, and an open floor plan that make for a comfortable weekend retreat. The plan combines kitchen, dining, and living areas into one spacious, comfortably informal room.

The exterior brick walls and a slate-shingled tower from which the fire hoses were hung and dried were all that was standing. The two fire-truck bays, marked by brick arches, were cleverly turned into a front porch by recessing the front wall by about 6 ft. The granite tracks that lead to each opening are now decorative—a visual echo of the carriage ruts that would have been there a hundred years ago.

French doors set into in the right bay bring light into the interior. With about 1,500 sq. ft. to work with, the architect made the most of the space by combining functions. The living, dining, and kitchen areas are open, creating a spacious first floor. A short hallway leads to a bedroom with full bath, a furnace utility room, and the stairs that lead to the second floor.

Upstairs are two sleeping areas, one a bedroom with half-bath and the second provided by a balcony that's open to the lower level. The tower has been transformed into a study that's accessible from the bedroom; a ladder goes to the top floor, a room just big enough for one person.

While the weekend home is still called the "firehouse," there are no fire engines or any other common forms of transportation. The island boasts a no-vehicle policy. People either walk or get around in electric golf carts, which the owners park out back. ✦

A second-level mezzanine area, **which doubles as a sleeping loft, creates a lower ceiling in the kitchen and dining areas.**

The two fire-truck bays, marked by brick arches, were cleverly turned into a front porch by recessing the front wall by about 6 ft.

Making the Most of the Floor Plan

Garage living is usually defined by a small amount of square footage. To make the most of this limited space, it's best to keep the area open, particularly between kitchen and living areas. The challenge is to create separate areas within this open space.

Ceiling height is one way to define different areas. The higher ceiling space is usually allocated to the public areas, while a sloped ceiling can define private areas like bedrooms. Kitchens are best located in perimeter space.

The alcove is also a way to differentiate function within a larger space. An alcove is literally a small area that's defined within a larger space. Window seats create alcoves, as do certain kinds of dormers; an alcove can even be created by movable screens. Alcoves can be big enough for a bed, defining a sleeping area within a larger living space. Or they can be small enough to create a space just for one: an office area, reading area, exercise space, or a place to listen to music or watch television.

The Family Garage

THE ATTACHED GARAGE THAT ARCHITECT Abraham Kadushin designed for the Linkner family holds two cars and two teenagers. Unlike most garage additions, this one did not replace an existing garage—a small garage still stands in the backyard.

The need for more bedroom space, especially for teenagers, inspired the idea of a garage addition that would be separate yet connected with the rest of the house. The advantages of adding an attached garage were both practical and aesthetic. The addition, which creates three new bedrooms, could not have been achieved in the house without considerably altering its form. The garage, which is connected to the house but very much its own structure, extends the design of the house without really changing its original form.

The primary design challenge for the architect was the narrowness of the city lot. "We wanted the garage to flank the house so that it could function as part of the house, but the amount of space was just under 13 ft. wide. There seemed to be only one way to go." And that was up. Kadushin designed a narrow, three-level garage addition in keeping with the house's Arts and Crafts style. The arched window

The garage extends the design of the house without really changing its original form.

This three-level garage addition puts cars on the ground floor and teenagers on the second and third levels. Kadushin designed the addition to complement but not overwhelm the Arts and Crafts house. The arched window, siding, and steep roof are inspired by the house.

on the second level is inspired by the covered entrance to the home's front door. The shingle pattern responds directly to the house, and the steep pitch of the garage quotes the dormer window on the house's third floor.

A place all its own

The garage is stepped back so that it becomes its own structure, not merely an extension of the house. Ground level is all garage, but the narrowness of the site prohibited parking cars side by side. Two sets of garage doors, one in back and one streetside, allow the owners to park linearly.

The architect designed seamless connections from garage to house on the first and second levels. A mudroom connects the parking area of the garage to the kitchen, a useful addition in this northern climate. On the second level, Kadushin extended an existing stair landing to become a sort of bridge between the house and the two bedrooms and bath in the new garage quarters. A ladder stair in the back bedroom leads upstairs to a loft, which serves the family as a play area and extra bedroom when needed.

Plenty of storage and built-ins help save space. The stair landing features built-in bookcases, and each bedroom has a window seat with storage below and built-in bookshelves. ✦

The Mudroom Connector

In many homes, the connection between the garage and the mudroom is the most-used entrance to the house. Not only will family members arriving in a vehicle enter the house through the garage, but also those on foot—if they're coming home from school or in from the backyard. To that end, the entrance should be as functional as it can be, as well as pleasant and welcoming.

A mudroom is like an anteroom between the garage and house (usually the kitchen), which also serves as a collection area for everything from boots to recycling. It's the drop-off area for books, briefcases, backpacks, and sports equipment—all of which can conspire to create a jumbled mess of a room. But a mudroom connecting the garage to the house can really be a useful addition, especially in a colder climate.

The design of a mudroom should take into account windows, views, and the quality of light, as well as the experience of entering and exiting the home. The accumulation of things that get dropped off in the mudroom should be addressed by built-ins or other carefully conceived storage solutions such as benches, cubbies, hooks and pegs, and ample countertop space.

The two bedrooms **on the second level each benefit from a window and a built-in window seat. The ladder in the photo leads to a loft area, which can be used either as a spare bedroom or as a playroom.**

The elegant arched **window is a detail that visually connects the garage addition with the house; inside, it gives an elegant focal point to the room.**

Defining the height of the kneewall is very important to the scale, proportion, and use of the space.

Kneewalls in the Garage

The second floor of a garage is not unlike an attic. The pitch of the roof creates a high ceiling that slopes down to the edge of the room. That outside edge of the room is defined by kneewalls, those short walls (typically about 3 ft. to 4 ft.) found between the floor and the sloping roof.

Defining the height of the kneewall is very important to the scale, proportion, and use of the space. Essentially, kneewall placement is ruled by the need to maximize a room's usable space without going too low (unless the attic is an A-frame, in which case you can't use the edges of the space anyway). A kneewall that's too high or that comes too far into the room wastes space in the perimeter and defeats the charm of living in the roof.

THE KNEEWALL

Placement of kneewalls defines the proportion, scale, and usability of a room. If it's too close to the outside wall of the house, the space at the perimeter becomes less useful and the ceiling is too low for furniture or any kind of access. If the kneewall is too far into the room, valuable space is wasted and the walls become so tall that you lose a sense of proportion and scale. At the right position, kneewalls offer space for built-ins, beds, and desks.

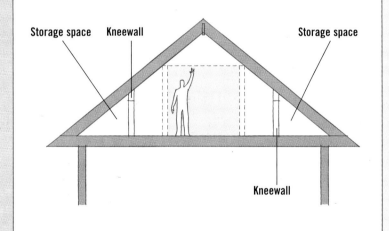

Storage space   Kneewall   Storage space

Kneewall

And a kneewall always creates a channel of space that can be used for storage. With doors or shelves built in, kneewall storage uses space that wouldn't have been used for anything else. It's a great solution for storage in a small space.

Boats, Cars, and Guests

The cottage offers a safe haven for boats through one end and cars through the other.

IT SEEMS AS IF THE DRIVEWAY to this building is made of water. In fact, this guest cottage doubles as both a garage for boats and for cars. Sited lakeside, the cottage offers a safe haven for boats through one end and cars through the other.

Designed by Bill Holtz of Bensonwood Homes, the boathouse is part of a family complex that sits on the shores of a large New Hampshire lake. Its owners have a collection of canoes and boats, including a war canoe that's big enough for 10 people. They wanted a place that could store boats and also serve as a private place for guests, particularly visiting family members.

The boathouse combines all these functions: It's deep enough to store that very long canoe, house a workshop for boats, and provide parking space for guests' cars and boat trailers. For park-

From the lake, **the garage/boathouse welcomes visitors who travel by water. On land, the boathouse functions as a garage, workshop, and complete guest house. A stepped window pattern allows stunning views of the lake.**

Inside, a soaring pattern of windows brings sweeping views of the lake. The outside deck was designed to be like "the prow of a boat," says architect Bill Holtz. The great room combines living, eating, and cooking functions in one open space.

ing, there's a drive-through garage, behind the boat slips.

Upstairs, accommodations include a great room with kitchen and dining areas, with a soaring ceiling and sweeping views of the lake, and a bedroom and bath toward the back of the structure. A sleeping loft that opens to the great room can sleep several children.

The boathouse and the house it accompanies are stunning examples of timberframe construction, which is a method of building that literally shows off the "wooden bones" of the structure. The interior finish wood used for the boathouse is similar to that used in the house—clear Douglas fir and Port Orford cedar. The cedar, which is actually from the cypress family and is white, is as strong as fir, light as pine, and is fitting for a boathouse, as it's a wood used in boatbuilding. ◆

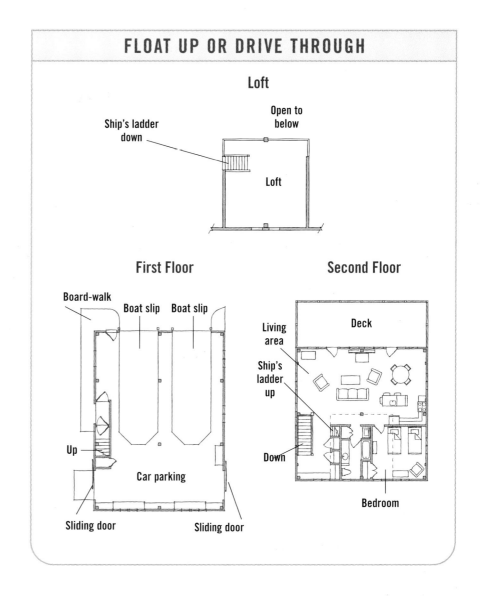

FLOAT UP OR DRIVE THROUGH

Loft

Ship's ladder down

Open to below

Loft

First Floor

Board-walk

Boat slip   Boat slip

Up

Car parking

Sliding door   Sliding door

Second Floor

Deck

Living area

Ship's ladder up

Down

Bedroom

This garage goes by the name "Barnage," a subtle salute to the structure's barnish facade. Two bays hold a woodshop and car; the shed off to the side was planned to minimize the facade of the garage and to echo a New England tradition of adding on to older buildings.

The Barnage

CHARLES MILLER, WHOSE DAY JOB is executive editor for *Fine Homebuilding* magazine, brought his expertise as a designer and craftsman to the creation of his garage. Designated the "Barnage" in salute to its abstract barnish facade, Miller's garage on last visit had everything in it but cars. Downstairs, in one bay, a thriving woodshop threatens to take up even more space; upstairs, the apartment intended for visitors is elegantly finished with hand-cast concrete and custom-built niches and nooks.

The house the garage accompanies is a log house, circa 1986, which Miller says is perfectly sited on its wooded lot but "had very

The plan of the Barnage created a courtyard area by having the garage offset from the house. Set back so it doesn't block light, the garage helps define the exterior space. The two deck levels create an entrance, which is covered with wisteria in the warmer months. The door leads to an interior stairwell that takes you up to the "Clubhouse."

little charm when we bought it." One of its design flaws, in his mind, is a roof that manages to be half-gambrel and half-gable. Part of the rationale behind the siting of the garage proved to be a way to mask that offensive roofline.

The garage sits where it needs to, according to local setback requirements. And its placement to the side, slightly overlapping the house, accomplishes three things: It blocks the roofline, it allows daylight into the side windows of the house, and it creates a wall for an outdoor courtyard in the back of the house.

Cutting cost without cutting corners

Working on the weekends, Miller spent three years and $20,000 building his garage. It features the best material from the salvage and recycled pile: The wood to frame it was purchased in reject units, the windows are second-hand, the interior finish wood—oak and hemlock—bought at a fire sale. Even the paint was a deal, purchased from Home Depot's "Goof Collection," the gallons of paint that get returned because they're the wrong color. As he says, "There are no bad colors, just bad combinations of colors."

The room upstairs is where Miller gathers with friends to play music or to be alone to work on illustrations or writing projects for the magazine. Small and efficient, it manages to combine three spaces into one: the overall living area, centered by a hand-cast concrete fireplace; a work alcove, which is plumbed for

The mantel is cast from concrete.
Its mold is made from wiggle board, the material that roofers lay down prior to nailing on corrugated roofing. The form above the fireplace is cast from a three-part mold. Notice how the lines start to blend in the middle, creating a "smoke effect." Built-ins help save precious square footage: the television, stereo equipment, firewood, and amplifier all have their own niche.

kitchen functions should the need ever arise; and a full bath. It also serves as the home's guest room.

Built-ins help conserve space. The bookshelf is code height and doubles as a stair railing; niches hold the television, stereo, guitar amplifier, and firewood; and a shelf unit, handcrafted from the same hemlock that lines the peaked ceiling, helps distinguish the office area from the rest of the room.

Close to the house yet somehow far away, the Barnage, Miller says, manages to be a slice of Vermont in Connecticut. It's become an everyday getaway for its designer and builder—the space, he proclaims, "that's the best room in the house." ◆

The built-in bookcase is code height and doubles, on the other side, as a stair rail. Plenty of windows, all of them purchased secondhand, let in lots of light; a ventilating skylight contributes to the quality of both light and air.

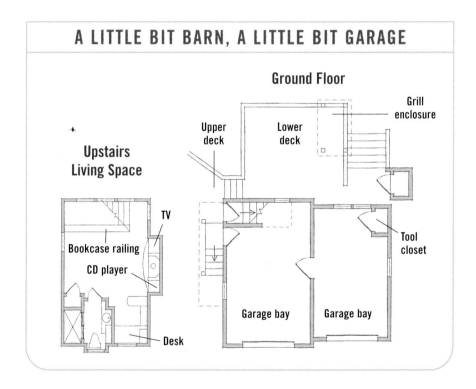

A LITTLE BIT BARN, A LITTLE BIT GARAGE

Ground Floor

Grill enclosure

Upper deck

Lower deck

Upstairs Living Space

TV

Bookcase railing

CD player

Tool closet

Desk

Garage bay

Garage bay

Design Challenges and Solutions

The challenges
◆ Create guest room, getaway, and garage in one
◆ Use Barnage to camouflage log home
◆ Maximize use of single upstairs room

The solutions
◆ Design two-bay garage with guest room above
◆ Design building to be template for home remodel
◆ Create multizoned room above

The interior squeezes the most from limited space **by keeping the plan open and designating different functions architecturally. The peaked ceiling contributes to the feeling of spaciousness. The central area is where people gather to play music. It's also the guest room for the house and a home office for Miller.**

The garage doors are custom-built from Spanish cedar, a hardwood from the mahogany family. Transom windows let light into the first level, while the cupola on the top brings sunlight into the upper level.

A 200-year-old timberframe barn in Maine was transformed into a garage that doubles as a guest house. The size of the original barn was extended with a shed for parking the car. The main structure can also hold vehicles, although its first level is in service as a playroom and storage area.

Barn Quarters

THE BARN IS A NOT-SO-DISTANT relative of the garage. (Although the garage is less suited for holding farm animals, both shelter mechanical equipment.) In this instance, a 200-year-old timberframe barn has been converted into a garage for cars as well as expansive guest quarters for people.

Builder and designer John Libby scours the Maine countryside for old barns, which his company dismantles and then restores. This barn, entirely restored, was moved to coastal Maine, where it joined an existing house and another barn, already in service as a farm-equipment garage.

The clients wanted more space for parking as well as a guest house with its own bath and kitchen facilities. Two garage spaces were added: in a shed built as an extension to the barn and in the barn itself, which is also outfitted with garage doors. Finished inside with exposed timberframe and wide pine boards, the space intended for cars is now in use as a playroom. Guests stay upstairs in living quarters that include two bedrooms and a common shared sitting area. The cupola, not original to the barn, brings light into the living area. ✦

Upstairs, the two bedrooms, which are finished in exposed beams and clapboard, have been insulated for year-round living. Radiant heat helps keep the inside warm during the winter months.

The covered entrance **leads to this small foyer, in which one door leads into the garage and stairs lead to the upstairs apartment. The closet under the stairs features a door of rich cherry wood, which echoes the kitchen cabinets upstairs. The floor and stair treads are red birch.**

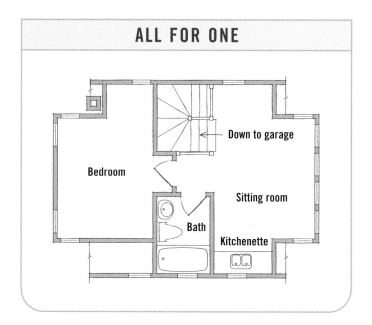

ALL FOR ONE

Bedroom

Down to garage

Sitting room

Bath

Kitchenette

An Elegant Garage for One

RICHARD BERNHARD KNOWS THE TRIALS of sharing living space with almost-teenagers. "The music," he says, "is so loud."

Newly divorced, he found himself wanting a different sort of house, one that would offer privacy and comfort for all family members. The model he looked to comes from the past—a house with a detached carriage house, with apartment on top.

"The idea was to look to old carriage houses and stables for inspiration. And to build a structure that would be nice enough to show clients," says Bernhard, who works as an architect in Maine.

So he started by designing the garage. The structure does, in fact, look as though it may be a converted carriage house. Sided in shingles and covered with a barn roof, the garage house nestles into its wooded setting.

A covered entrance opens to two doors: one that leads to the garage and the other to a stairway to the upstairs apartment. A generous one-and-a-half car parking area translates on the second level to about 450 sq. ft. Shed dormers on the west and east sides of the garage expand the space. Bernhard wanted the apartment to feel spacious, so he planned for higher than the usual 8-ft. ceilings.

The floor plan is divided into two areas, a bedroom that faces west and a living area with a small kitchenette. Each area feels big, because it is, in truth,

The architect who lives in this elegant little garage intends to use the building as a design influence for the house to come. With live-in quarters upstairs, the garage looks to the old-fashioned carriage house as inspiration. The garage doors are standard issue, made special by applying wood battens to the surface.

Inside the upstairs apartment, details like red-birch floors and lots of windows create an elegant, airy interior. The sitting area also functions as a dining room and home office.

A kitchenette is tucked into a niche off the sitting area and can be hidden entirely from view by a screen.

Design Challenges and Solutions

The challenges

- ✦ Create garage that looks like an old carriage house
- ✦ Provide private space for members of the family
- ✦ Provide room for cars

The solutions

- ✦ Add traditional touches such as shingle siding, cherry cabinets, red-birch flooring
- ✦ Add shed dormers and raise ceiling height to create more space
- ✦ Create separate areas for garage and apartment

good sized. The key to this small space is that each part shares various functions. The kitchen is tucked into a niche in the sitting area, while a workplace occupies a corner of the room.

Bernhard specified beautiful materials throughout, which lend elegance to the space. The floors are red birch; the kitchen cabinets are crafted from cherry. There are 21 windows in this small structure, which bring an airy, spacious feeling to the interior.

This garage is really a small house, which will eventually serve as a guest house for visiting family and friends. In the meantime, Bernhard enjoys the snug living quarters and, with his architectural office nearby, finds himself showing off his starter garage to clients. ✦

The key to this small space is that each part shares various functions.

Where others feared to build,
architect Geoffrey Warner saw potential.
The narrow space seemed almost impossible
for a useful design. But, with care, an empty
parking space became a chance to expand the
house to include a master suite, with home
office and walkout deck.

A bridge — fabricated by the architect
from translucent corrugated fiberglass, exposed
fir studs, stainless-steel cable with nautical turn-
buckle fittings, and beveled mahogany planks cut
2 in. thick—connects the second level of the
house to the upstairs addition. On one side of the
bridge is a large walk-in closet and on the other
a small home office. (See the photos at right and
on the facing page.)

Attached Garage
with Bedroom Suite

THE WAY TOM ROSEN SEES THINGS, it's the garage that brought
light into his living room. Not only that, it added an extra bedroom, home office, and walkout deck, as well as covered parking.

Engineering such a feat of domestic daring was Geoffrey Warner,
a residential architect accustomed to turning apparently impossible sit-
uations into stylish, innovative design. The constraints of Rosen's long,
narrow city lot allowed room for only a one-car garage, which went

The addition is long and narrow, **which allows for an easy separation of space with the bedroom on one end, flanked by custom-made built-in storage, and a walkout balcony on the other.**

into an impossibly tight spot flanking the house. It's what happened on top of the garage that transformed the interior.

The house, a Victorian-era cottage, features charming small rooms that together create a cozy living environment. But what Rosen needed most was more space—specifically, a larger master bedroom and a home office, which were added atop the garage. Warner took what was once a small attic and turned it into a bridge passageway that connects the original house with the addition. The bridge adds visual interest downstairs and allows light from a second-level skylight to pour into the first-floor living and dining areas.

Upstairs, the bedroom runs the length of the garage; long and narrow, it has room for a bed, small sitting area, walk-in closet, and a home office tucked into a corner. Beyond the French doors, the living space is expanded, at least in warmer months, onto a balcony that overlooks the front garden.

For one short period of time, Rosen considered only adding the garage to the house. "But once the foundation was poured and the structure planned, it seemed like a waste not to finish it off—and give the house the extra space it needs to function well." ✦

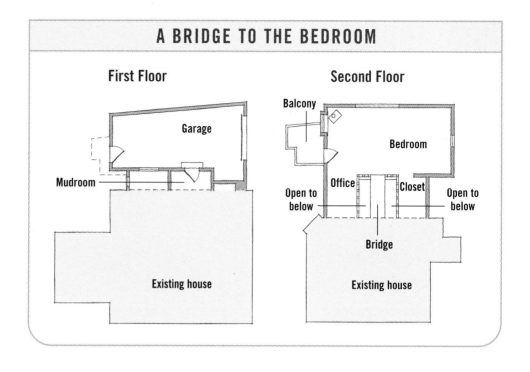

A BRIDGE TO THE BEDROOM

First Floor

Balcony · Garage · Mudroom · Existing house

Second Floor

Bedroom · Office · Closet · Open to below · Open to below · Bridge · Existing house

The constraints of Rosen's long, narrow city lot allowed room for only a one-car garage, which went into an impossibly tight spot flanking the house.

Parking in the Garage

THE GARAGE WAS ORIGINALLY CONCEIVED, designed, and built as a place to park the car. It's American ingenuity that has turned it into the place where we seem to do everything but.

The car was a thing of beauty when it first drove onto the scene and, as such, deserved nice digs. Landscape historian J. B. Jackson, in one of the few written essays devoted to garages, suggests that there are three distinct phases in the evolution of the garage. The first, the romantic phase, came at a time when the car itself was a breath of luxury and style. The next is the practical stage, exemplified by all those generic, unattractive garages that line alleys and streets in every American city. The last stage he calls "the family garage," which encompasses those garages where there's space to include any kind of family activity. Jackson wrote his essay in the mid 1970s. Who knows what he might make of today's megagarage, the structure designed to

This garage **both services and shows off classic automobiles.**

This megagarage **parks up to 20 cars—each and every one has been restored by its owner to gleaming perfection.**

From the yard, this garage looks like a small cottage, but its function is to park the car.

house the car that's actually bigger than the house itself.

Today, garages tend to impress with girth, not with wit; they've been described as "garages on steroids." They are the structural equivalent of the stretch limo—impossibly large, with only some semblance of their original function in evidence.

Some big garages manage to combine size with substance. And to distinguish them from the run of the mill "garage-mahal," designers have elevated them to "carriage houses." While the carriages these carriage houses contain are horseless (primarily), they manage to capture the elegance of the past, while including every convenience of the present.

A multistory parking garage in Miami reminds us of an era when the cars were big and there was always plenty of parking.

THE GARAGE MECHANIC

*T*he word garage began to be used in the early 1900s to describe the place cars go to be repaired. The reason was that the garage—the one out back—was, at least in the first decade of the automobile, the place where the chauffeur worked on the car. (Yes, the chauffeur—with a fancy French name that translates into "fireman," because of the early flammable nature of autos.)

The chauffeur was a person of many talents, and the garage a place for many activities, among them the storage of gasoline. While the chauffeur is no longer the person who works on the transmission, the garage is still the place to take a car in need of repair.

And if you can't get closure from your customary garage mechanic, there's always the radio. Among America's lauded (and humorous) mechanics are Tom and Ray Magliozzi, who answer car owners' questions on National Public Radio. The problems they are willing to tackle range from the practical to the personal.

This garage promises **a "square deal"—the car repair shop's equivalent to a square meal.**

Diana Phillips, a 27-year-old auto mechanic, chose to rent a friend's garage to start her auto-repair business and to dedicate it to honesty, hard work, and doing right by the customer. While Phillips is quick to admit that most of the people she finds working in repair shops are male, she does not view herself as anything more than a good mechanic who specializes in Japanese cars. After apprenticing with a Quaker mechanic with leftist leanings, Phillips found herself wanting to avoid the factory-type atmosphere of larger service shops.

Beyond three garage doors, which lets her bring in more than one vehicle to service at a time, the decoration of her workspace involves little more than a boom box, tool box, gas heater, good lights, a couple of workbenches, and an air compressor.

Young mechanic at work: **Diana Phillips works on cars in a bare-bones rented garage.**

Beautiful Garages for Cars

Whether grand or modest, the garage is no longer just the garage, willing to wear the shabbiest of exteriors in service to a humble function. The garage is a place worthy of an architect's attention; a structure that can add to the worth of a home in the same way that the carriage house did in the last century.

A garage designed just for cars tends to be distinctive. Rarely does it blend into the house, nor is it hidden in the backyard. People who love cars tend to build temples to them. In my search for garages, I found one that is carpeted—not for the patter of little feet, but for an elderly MG, which is taken out only on the loveliest of days. Many garages are so clean that you can eat off the floor. The garage in some instances turns literally into a museum of cars or motorcycles, a place where they are kept and displayed.

The cars behind these garage doors range from sentimental favorites to one-of-a-kind vintage vehicles, which one car collector referred to as "rolling sculptures." The garages to follow aren't merely "mega"; they've been designed to provide an elegant backdrop, to be a witty counterpart or a striking conversation piece.

These garages are good-looking on the outside but have a fair amount of attention paid to their interiors. Anyone who collects cars spends time in the garage, which often is outfitted with the comforts of home: bathrooms, sitting areas, and offices. There seems to be a connection between the niceness of the cars and the extravagance of the garage, and one enterprising designer included in this chapter decided that the house should be the place to put the car. His "garage" is the living room.

There's an increased awareness on the part of designers and garage owners that the garage is a structure worthy of good design.

GARAGE ARCHITECTURE

*T*he development of architecture for various modes of transportation (planes and trains, for example) has a grand history that is about movement, about passage and human progress. Garages, which hold our primary method of transportation, don't share that grand architectural history. The architecture of a garage, if it has any, is rarely solely about the car: It either tends to extend the house, as if the car were really an occupant, or to ignore the structure altogether by putting it out back.

Frank Lloyd Wright was among the first architects to design houses that proudly displayed the car. Wright claimed that he invented the carport, which put the car on full view. Other architects over ensuing decades have tried to find a way to express artistically the way our culture relies on the car. These garages aren't visually camouflaged by the house but instead add to the expression of the house.

The architecture of a garage is rarely solely about the car.

Architect Frank Lloyd Wright designed this horse barn, which reflects the then-prevalent notion that the horse should be treated like a gentleman. Ten years after it was built in 1894, the owners converted the stable into a temporary garage—half cars, half horses.

This garage, which was designed by architect David Salmela, isn't simply a place to park cars. Take the automobiles out and the garage doubles as an amphitheater.

Designed to look like an elegant garage, the Allen Motorcycle Museum (above and left) holds a collection of vintage racing and touring motorcycles from 1955 to the present.

For the most part, garages designed for parking the car make function their ruling principle, and function in this instance means space that is well lit and easily accessible. And the need for a garage can lead to some surprisingly creative solutions, such as two enterprising neighbors, neither with room for a garage or a driveway of their own: Their solution? A two-stall garage, with a driveway between the two houses, which the neighbors share.

A lot of garages are for parking the Toyota and the Taurus, but a surprising number are a lot more. There's an increased awareness on the part of designers and garage owners that the garage is a structure worthy of good design. Its form adds to the design of the property, and its function is easily changeable, with the right planning. In other words, what holds cars today may well house an elderly relative in the future.

The garages in this chapter are for cars. Many are architect-designed, and all of them were built to be an important, and in some instances the preferred, part of the house. ✦

Dressing Up the Garage

When it first made its appearance in the backyard, the garage was considered an asset, not an eyesore. Of course, the first people to build garages were wealthy and so their garages were usually as grand as the accompanying house or carriage house. Even middle-class garages had either charm or novelty (mostly both) going for them and were designed to blend with the existing architecture of the house. The more functional aspects of the garage, such as the door, were often disguised by garden elements, pergolas, trellises, and screens.

Newer garages, which are by necessity and desire bigger, can create a challenge to any yard. A wall of garage doors in the front of the house can put the worst part of the house forward, while the side of a large garage offers a blank wall to the backyard.

Such blank walls can be an inspiration for a variety of decorative elements. A Midwestern couple, who collect art for the interior of their home, enlisted sculptor Irve Dell to make a piece of art for the garden, using the garage's wall as a blank canvas. Dell worked with a variety of materials, among them bronze, wood, and glass, to bring focus to the wall. Using a garden motif, he played off certain architectural elements of the house—a window and a window seat, balanced by a bronze trellis.

Consider every garage door **or exterior wall as a blank canvas, especially if it faces the yard.**

This 1921 Craftsman-style bungalow had all the right lines, which the owner exaggerated to create the sort of space he envisioned. The ceiling was heightened, the door replaced with a series of French doors, and the driveway constructed in such a way as to lead right into the living room.

Park the Car… in the Living Room

JIM HULL IS THINKING ABOUT his next garage. His new home, which will be built in Malibu, will have a pond, and by the pond will be a large, gorgeous garage, with many garage doors, all opening pond-side. He has a vision: the cars parked on the lawn, facing the water—a sort of automotive reflecting pool.

This scene—watching the sun set over a body of water before a group of dazzling vintage cars—is not the romantic daydream of a

car fanatic. It is, rather, part of Hull's ongoing homage to the beauty of the automobile.

Hull, who trained as an architect and urban designer at the Massachusetts Institute of Technology, has spent his career pursuing good design. To Hull, a beautifully designed car is on the same level as a work of fine sculpture. His collection of rare French Delahayes, designed in the 1930s and '40s, are marvels of steel, Plexiglas, and rare woods. Back when his collection of these cars numbered as many as 25, he wanted an environment that would showcase the cars as works of art.

That place, in his former Brentwood residence, turned out not to be the garage but the living room. A car in the living room may sound way out, but Hull, tired of the constant gender segregation during parties, as the men trooped to the garage to admire the cars and the women stayed in the house, determined to bring the cars home, into the house, where everybody could enjoy them.

His 1921 Craftsman bungalow, before renovation, had essentially a U-shaped floor plan. By enclosing the patio to create a new center of the house, adding a high ceiling to create a great room, and making sure the doors were wide enough, Hull brought his garage inside.

Hull was determined to show off the car in such a way that viewers could see it as it was originally created—at eye-level. An old-fashioned hydraulic lift proved to be the necessary equipment, so it was installed in the great room where the car could be admired from all directions.

There's a hush, says Hull, that comes over a group of car lovers when faced with an automobile of particular beauty. The moment before the lift went up, Hull would open the doors to the great room, drive the car inside, and as the car began to ascend, the party would start. ✦

The vintage 1937 **French Talbot-Lago coupe rests in the living room atop its own hydraulic lift. The homeowner, who collects classic automobiles, wanted to spend more quality time with his favorite cars.**

By enclosing the patio, adding a high ceiling, and making sure the doors were wide enough, Hull brought his garage inside.

A classic 1948 French-made Delahaye automobile and **a bright yellow 1965 Ferrari naturally become the most vivid conversation pieces in the living room of this California home.**

Wanted: One-Car Garage

It's not fancy, but then it only cost its owner $1. Moved to its location and renovated, the garage was a cost-effective solution to a parking problem. The total tab, after moving, roofing, electrical work, and window installation, was close to $1,000.

THE AD READ: "WANTED: ONE-CAR GARAGE, will move." Mary Titus, an enterprising college professor, placed the ad in her town's newspaper because her 1900 house was missing a garage. Four people responded. Titus then embarked on a tour of garages, some of which, she recalls, "were nothing more than chicken shacks."

The garage she bought was of an early vintage; the roof was rotted, and it needed painting. But the price was right at $1. Titus was certain she couldn't go wrong. Of course, a $1 garage isn't useful if it's in someone else's yard, so a house-moving company was enlisted to move the garage to her backyard. After pouring a concrete foundation, the garage was delivered and carefully placed at the end of the driveway. Titus and her family reroofed it, wired it, and painted it. And then they parked.

But then, discontent set in—the garage was too dark. It needed windows. But a solution was soon found. The storm windows sitting in the basement were enlisted, holes were cut in the garage walls, and then there was light. ◆

THE BATCAVE: A MULTITASK GARAGE, AT HEART

The Batcave started out in the early 1940s as an old barn.

All devotees of Batman—in the chronicles, on television, and more recently in the movies—have admired the Batmobile, "A black thunderbolt on wheels," so described in the March 1956 chronicle *Secrets of the Batmobile*. But what makes this thunderbolt even more impressive is the luxurious home it has found in the Batcave.

The Batcave started out in the early 1940s as an old barn. The addition of a batplane created a need for more space, and the best way to go proved to be down. Over the years, and in various different media, the Batcave has expanded to include three levels of subterranean caverns, each filled with an important and ever-changing roster of crime-fighting necessities. The fire pole was added in the mid-1950s, when Batman and Robin were involved in "fire-prevention week" and were responding not only to calls of peril and crime but also to fire alarms.

The Batcave (and Batman) made it to television in 1966: The show, starring Adam West, imagined the Batcave—and the Batmobile—outfitted with the latest in technology.

In its more recent film interpretations, the Batcave is a looming, cavernous space that somehow manages to be the garage equivalent of the Gothic mansion where Bruce Wayne resides.

The Batcave **as it appeared in 1968 on the ABC-TV series** *Batman*. **It's large enough for a mod convertible Batmobile and the latest in crime-fighting equipment.**

French Country Garage

The garage has become almost part of the house—small square windows look out into the garden courtyard, while the garage doors are hidden from view on the other side. By incorporating the garage into the footprint of the house the architect maximized usable space. On top, the second floor contains office space and bedrooms.

THERE ARE TWO GARAGES ON THIS Midwestern country estate: one, an attached garage that holds the family vehicles; the other, a carriage house that serves as a sentinel to the home.

Designed by Dan Nepp of TEA₂ for clients who collect cars, the garage and carriage house are dominant elements on this property. "Putting the garage at the front of the house is something our firm tries to avoid," says Nepp. "But with this particular project, garages were used in a unique way to define the estate feel of the house and to develop the courtyard."

The house itself is literally half garage. A courtyard was created by placement of the carriage house and the attached garage. The architect gave both garages architectural details more befitting a house, such as window boxes and dormer windows, and hid

A vintage 1920s gas pump out front hints at the building's function—a carriage house, intended to hold a collection of cars. The garage doors, designed by the building's architect, were custom built. They swing out and have locking bolts that keep them open while cars come and go.

A view of the carriage house from the courtyard—it stands sentinel, almost like a welcoming cottage. The building is actually three stories high; the lowest level is tucked into a slope and is accessible by another driveway.

garage doors from public view. The three-story carriage house looks like a cottage on the property; with three 1,000-sq.-ft. levels, it's house-sized, though the lower level is set into a hill to minimize its scale. The first two floors are used for workshop space and car storage, while the top is intended for a getaway or guest house. ◆

Garage Doors

An ugly garage door on a stylish garage is the equivalent of a fashion faux pas: It ruins the overall effect. Yet in the world of budget decisions, the custom garage door is often the first to go, because a custom door can cost twice as much (or more) as a stock model. But in some newer houses, the garage door is on the same side of the house as the front door and has become,

The three doors in this garage **don't overwhelm the structure because they were designed and constructed with special care to match the garage itself. In case you can't tell how these doors work, notice the slight seams between individual panels—these are actually overhead doors.**

at least for the people who live there, the entrance they use every day.

The garage door deserves as much attention in this instance as the front door, and architects often design the two doors with the same details. If budget is an issue, there are ways to embellish a standard door with finish carpentry: Simple, added trim can be a cost-efficient way to add character.

The first garage doors were made from wood and usually swung open. Other popular early models included doors that folded up like an

accordion and doors that slid from side to side on tracks. But it was the introduction of a door that could (especially with the touch of a button) fold up in sections overhead, that created a new world of convenience. The world of illusion is alive and well in garage-door design: The type of door that swings out is still popular, only manufacturers now make it to just look that way—it folds up like other overhang doors.

High-end, new garage doors **tend to look like they're old. Mostly made from wood, with glass panels, these "designer doors" do more to finish off a garage than any other item. This garage door has a built-in people entrance.**

It always looks better **to have two single doors than one double door, but if the doors must be double, try to make them look like two singles. It breaks up the expanse of space, making the facade of the garage more visually appealing.**

Civilized Parking

BOSTON ARCHITECT JEREMIAH ECK designed this garage for a professional couple who live in a pricey area of the city. When their original garage, from an earlier, less distinguished time, blew apart during Hurricane Bob in the late 1980s, the clients were interested in adding a new garage that would contribute to the value of the property. They determined to rebuild, this time giving the garage some distinction.

The house itself is Victorian. Eck took his lead from that period, but the shape and scope came from the clients' desire to have a three-car garage and a working bay that was tall enough for a car lift.

"The difficulty with a four-car garage is that you have to deal with four garage doors without modulation," Eck said. His design provides that modulation in the roofline and in the arch, which sets back three of the doors from the face of the garage. ✦

This four-car garage is designed to provide parking for three cars and to include a working bay for car repair with a two-story lift. The working bay is under the peaked roof. The three garage doors are recessed, which helps relieve the visual tension people feel when the "gaping mouth of a garage door sits flat against the garage wall," the architect says.

Making a Big Garage Better

With the current passion for sports utility vehicles, what would ordinarily be a large garage suddenly isn't big enough. The largest of the SUVs has forced the standard garage door from its current 8 ft. wide by 7 ft. high to about 9 ft. square, so the driver can park without having to first get out of the car and fold in the mirrors.

The space allotted to park the car is usually larger than the square footage for a child's bedroom. Standard interior depth is 22 ft.; each bay needs to be about 8 ft. wide with another 4 ft. clearance all around. Long cars measure in at about 16 ft., which leaves about 6 ft. at the front of the garage for storage or a workbench.

As garages get bigger (many have four or five bays and tend to be as big as the house they accompany), often little attention is paid to their design. However, certain design considerations can transform what could look like a barn into a garage worthy of the house it accompanies. For instance, in a three-car garage, what will that third bay do? Some people think they need it for the eventuality of a third car (for the 6-year-old who will be a teenager someday), or they need storage for a boat or sports car. If that third stall is intended for anything other than a car, however, you can safely reduce the size of the bay by a few feet and eliminate the third garage door.

A standard three-car garage creates a 36-ft. plane, which is usually longer than any wall in the house. Here are a few ways to minimize the scale:

✦ Visually scale down the third bay by setting it back from the front of the garage and giving it its own, smaller roof.

✦ Never use a double door for the other bays; use two single doors instead.

✦ If the door has to be 16-ft. wide, design it so that it looks like two doors. The smaller scale of each door will impart a less barnlike look to the garage even if the square footage is unchanged.

As garages get bigger, often little attention is paid to their design.

REDUCING THE SCALE

If you're uncomfortable with having a garage that seems to dwarf your house, many options exist for downplaying the scale of anything larger than a two-car garage. Here are two possible solutions.

Solution 1

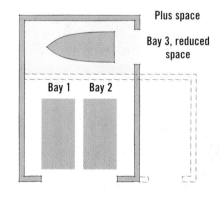

Plus space

Bay 3, reduced space

Bay 1   Bay 2

Solution 2

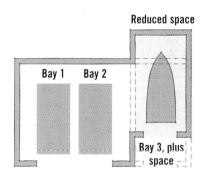

Reduced space

Bay 1   Bay 2

Bay 3, plus space

A Garage Storm

ARCHITECT BRENT RICHARDS NOT ONLY provided a garage design for Alex Meade and Clarissa Spawn, he offered up a 75-year-old pin oak from his property that had fallen in a storm.

Meade and Spawn live in a historic neighborhood in Kentucky, notable for its wide variety of architectural styles, from Federal to Craftsman. Even though the neighborhood is rife with historic homes, the city council had just passed a strict zoning law that changed the allowable height of secondary structures from 35 ft. to 15 ft., the standard suburban height for garages.

The carport works well **in the warm Kentucky climate, protecting the cars from heat and rain while doubling as a party patio. The collection of cars Meade parks in the garage and carport are historic—a 1957 MG, a 1961 Austin Healey bug-eyed sprite, and a 1960 VW bus.**

Shed Storage

Designed and built by a Rhode Island contractor, this garage offers many functions to the house it accompanies—including four parking spots, storage for the owner's contracting business, and a drying room for homemade sausage. But probably the most ingenious feature is the shed storage.

The garage hides the parking from view of the house and instead puts a people-scaled entrance and two arched storage bays on the courtyard. Beattie's idea for the storage came about because he wanted to hide the garbage cans from view; he carved out two 4-ft.-deep and 10-ft.-wide spots and finished them with an elegant arch. To avoid the buildup of odors, the sheds are floored with osmose, an open decking material that's also bug resistant. One shed is saved for garbage; the other is used seasonally to hold firewood and garden equipment.

This garage **provides parking for four cars and people-sized openings for storage of garbage, recyclables, and garden equipment.**

Fifteen feet is not only the standard height of suburban garages, it's also the height of most ordinary kit garages. But the couple wanted a garage that worked with their house and within the context of its historic neighborhood. As Meade points out, "If we built a garage that fit the city council's restrictions, it would have looked like any kind of generic structure."

With plans in hand, Meade and Spawn determined to mount a case for their garage before the Board of Adjustment. "We wanted to make the point that these limits force architectural conformance, and dictate a garage more suited for a suburban development than for a historic neighborhood." Not only did they get a variance from the board, the couple went on to get the zoning law reversed. Subsequently, several architect-designed garages have been built in the neighborhood.

With designs approved and the law changed, Meade set about bringing plans into reality. The structure, which combines a carport with a garage, was built by Meade using salvaged windows and doors from various neighborhood renovations. The architect had specified rough-cut siding, which fortuitously came available when a storm downed an oak tree in his yard. Meade and a friend purchased the tree for $200. Half the tree covered the exterior of the 900-sq.-ft. garage, and the other half became oak beams in a friend's house. When another tree in the neighborhood came down, that became ceiling planks for the carport. ✦

This garage/carport was built from recycled windows, doors, and lumber salvaged from a 30,000-lb. oak tree that fell during a storm. The Craftsman style of the garage was designed to make it fit into a historic neighborhood.

Twenty-Car Garage

BARRY BRISKMAN STARTED COLLECTING cars before he could even drive, buying his first collectible car, a 1940 Buick Ltd. convertible sedan, when he was 12. In those early years, he recalls a succession of cars—none of which he was able to drive—all financed through various partnerships and deals with his dad.

In the five decades since that first investment, he's purchased and lovingly restored more than 40 cars, of which the "best of" might include a 1931 LaSalle Fleetwood seven-passenger touring car; a 1934 Packard Super 8 2/4 coupe, which he owned for 31 years; and a rare 1937 MG SA Charlesworth Tourer that was featured in the Hitchcock film *Rebecca*.

This megagarage holds 20 cars, an assortment of bikes, and a small collection of pedal cars, assembled over the years by a passionate car collector, who admits a preference for old MGs. The L-shape of the garage helps make the 4,000-sq.-ft. space feel smaller and ensures that the view from the house isn't entirely of garage doors.

Making room for 20 cars

It doesn't take a high level of mathematical sophistication to figure that there's a connection between the number of cars Briskman owns and the size of his garage, which at the moment contains 15 cars but can hold 20. Over the years, the need for garage space has inspired a couple of additions to a former house, the renovation of an original garage into a dining room, and a move to a house where Briskman knew he would have room to grow his garage.

This latest garage has 4,000 sq. ft. under one roof. Briskman designed the garage in an L shape, which creates a courtyard and

The "living room" of Barry Briskman's garage holds a large collection of automotive books, as well as every issue of *Automobile Quarterly*, every issue of the *Classic Car Weekly* since 1953, a group of early automobile books, and service manuals and parts books. The trophy cases contain a collection of prizes won, including Best in Class at Pebble Beach. "The minute collection of insignificant pedal cars," as Briskman puts it, has sentimental value—the oldest one was "restored" for his daughter in 1963.

Barry Briskman at home in his garage, which combines storage with a workshop area.

Briskman designed the garage in an L shape, which creates a courtyard and minimizes the scale of the garage so that it doesn't overwhelm the house.

minimizes the scale of the garage so that it doesn't overwhelm the house. With five sets of double doors, the garage easily holds 12 cars, and the adjoining workshop space can hold another 3 cars.

There's an office, where Briskman works and displays car-collecting memorabilia, and a sitting area, where he can peruse any issue of *Automobile Quarterly* since the first year of its publication. Briskman admits to spending most of his time out there, in this home not so far away from home. "It's like the house isn't even here," says Briskman. ✦

Good-Neighbor Garage

Joined at the "hip," this garage is a creative solution for a difficult parking situation.

THIS GARAGE IS ACTUALLY two garages for two houses. Joined at the "hip," it's a creative solution for a difficult parking situation.

The idea came from a small-town pastor who was frustrated with his tuck-under garage. The problem was that any new garage would dominate his backyard and might require removing a beloved tree. Given that the local building codes required a wide alley between his garage and a neighbor's property, the best solution seemed to be to put the garage on the edge of the property line.

When the minister discovered that his neighbor also needed a garage, the idea struck: They would build one together. Because there was only 24 ft. between their houses, a common drive would be necessary.

The driveway involved most of the negotiation: Snow removal and parking extra cars can be the stuff feuds are made of. The solution was to divide the garage on the property line, and to put a wide apron at the top of the drive, which allows easier parking and a wider back-up space. ✦

This two-car garage actually serves two houses. With a common drive between them, the two garages are clearly delineated with separate roofs, doors, power supplies, and walls that need upkeep. The solution saved both neighbors valuable yard space.

A New Carriage House for Carriages

The reason George and Sandy Nelson added a carriage and tack room to their house is simple: George drives a horse and carriage to work every day, and he needed a place at home to keep the carriages. Once at work, the inevitable question of where to park the horse and buggy is answered by a corral, attached to the office parking lot.

Nelson's home parking facilities were designed by Wayne Ferson of Intuitive Design in the form of a carriage house that complements the architecture of the house, which is a reproduction of a circa 1700 two-story Colonial. "The clients wanted something that looked like it belonged on the property. And we decided that the building should express the frame," says Ferson.

George Nelson, who commutes to work with a horse and buggy, says that he uses his garage and carriage house about the same amount. The garage holds two cars on top. It dips down a story on the other side; structurally supported with steel, the garage contains a stable for two horses on this lower level.

That frame proved to be post and beam, a method of building in which the structure is created with a self-supporting framework of timbers fastened with wooden connections. Ferson enlisted James Dole of Uptack Design as builder. Using the elements appropriate to the building method, the carriage house completes a historic complex and acts as an introduction to the property, with its arched entrance and long one-story form. Inside, Nelson keeps an Amish carriage, a surrey (with a fringe on top) he uses in the summer months, and a marathon

The carriage house and tack room that Wayne Ferson designed for George and Sandy Nelson were designed to complement a replica of an 18th-century flat-front Colonial house. The archway entrance, paved with cobblestone, leads to a courtyard where the carriages can turn around.

The arched entranceway **shows off the structure of post-and-beam construction. Hand-forged hardware is both functional and decorative.**

vehicle, for competitions; the tack room is used for saddles and equipment for the horses.

The horses are kept under the garage. While from the front the garage looks like a building for two cars, it's built on a steep slope. Underneath there are two horse stalls, which are accessible from behind and below. George Nelson owns a steel bridge-building business, and he suggested steel construction with a metal-pan floor for the garage, enough to support two vehicles.

The finishing details are in keeping with the Nelsons' passion for all things early American. The hardware was forged by a blacksmith in Maine, and the doors were handcrafted. ✦

The details **are all carefully considered to give the carriage house an authentic, historic feel. The roof is hand-split cedar shingles, the doors were all custom-built out of pine boards, and the hardware was hand-forged by Jim Kearney from Maine.**

Nelson keeps an assortment of horse-drawn vehicles **inside the carriage house, which are in use almost every day. Built with post-and-beam construction, the interior expresses the structure of the building.**

Credits

Photo courtesy ABC TV/The Kobal Collection—p. 183.

Photos © Sandy Agrafiotis; Architect: Benjamin Nutter, Topsfield, Mass.—pp. 135–137.

Photos © Archive Photo/American Stock—pp. 8 (top) and 21.

Photo courtesy Art Institute of Chicago—p. 177 (top).

Photos © Carolyn L. Bates—pp. 67 and 96–97.

Photo © Laurie Black—p. 115 (right).

Photo © James P. Blair/Corbis—p. 8 (bottom).

Photos © Mark Boisclair—pp. 172 and 192–194.

Photos © Del Brown; Architect: Lou Heiser—pp. 104–107.

Photos © Geoffrey Carr—pp. 32 and 38–40.

Photos © Diane Cook and Len Jenshel 2000—pp. 10 (bottom), 11, 17–19, 82–83, and 87.

Photo courtesy Corbis/Bettmann—p. 12 (bottom).

Photo courtesy Corbis/Underwood & Underwood—p. 12 (top).

Photos © Grey Crawford; Architect: Jim Hull—pp. 180–181.

Photos © John Danicic; Architect: Robert Gerloff, Minneapolis, Minn.—pp. 69–71.

Photos © davidduncanlivingston.com—p. 4 (top) [and 80] and 81.

Photos © davidduncanlivingston.com; Builder: Michael Ballou—pp. 62–64.

Photos © davidduncanlivingston.com; Architect: Claire Beasley, San Francisco, Calif.—pp. 58–59.

Photos © davidduncanlivingston.com; Builder: Louis McBride—pp. 52–53.

Photos © Lisa DeCasare; Architect: Richard Kawalek, Ohio—pp. 112–114.

Photo © Irve Dell—p. 179.

Photos courtesy Designer Doors—p. 187 (bottom left and right).

Photo © Jeremiah Eck; Architect: Jeremiah Eck, Boston, Mass.—p. 188.

Photo by Andy Engel, courtesy *Fine Homebuilding* magazine, © The Taunton Press, Inc.—p. 24.

Photos by Andy Engel, courtesy *Fine Homebuilding* magazine, © The Taunton Press, Inc.; Builder: Ken Troupe, Subury, Ont.—pp. 126–128.

Photos © John Fulker; Builder: John Farquhar, Vancouver, B.C.—pp. 60–61.

Photo © John Gauvin; Designer/Builder: John Stanek, Custom Builders, Inc., Peterborough, N.H.—p. 22.

Photos © Alan Geller; Architect: Kurt Lavenson, Lavenson Design, Calif.—pp. 72–74.

Photo © Philip Gould/Corbis—p. 27.

Photos © Tomiko Gumbleton; Architect: Tom Holleman—pp. 138–141.

Photos © Tomiko Gumbleton; Architect: Abraham Kadushin—pp. 150–151 and 153.

Photo © Dennis Hallinan/FPG International—p. 15.

Photos © Jerry Howard/Positive Images—pp. v, 4 (bottom), and 90.

Photo © Yoram Kahana/Shooting Star Photo Agency—p. 122.

Photos © Rob Karosis; Architect: Malcolm MacKenzie, Newton, Mass.—pp. 77–79.

Photos © Peter Kerze—pp. 28 and 176–177 (bottom).

Photo © Carol Kitman—p. 10 (top).

Photos © Mark Kozlowski Photography, Inc.; Architect: Merrall MacNeille, Cheshire, Mass.—pp. 91–93.

Photo © Richard Laffin, Richard Laffin Architects—p. 174 (top).

Photos © Mary Ludington—pp. 48–49, 54 (bottom), 55–56, 68 (and 182), 75, 108–109, 175 (bottom), and 195.

Photos © Mary Ludington; Designer: Dennis Brose, Period Design—pp. 100–103.

Photo © Mary Ludington; Architect: Dale Mulfinger, SALA Architects, Minneapolis, Minn.—p. 7.

Photos © Mary Ludington; Architect: Dan Nepp, TEA$_2$, Minneapolis, Minn.—pp. 20 (top) and 184–186.

Photos © Mary Ludington; Architect: Geoffrey Warner, Minneapolis, Minn.—pp. 168–170.

Photos courtesy Marshall Erdman & Associates; Architects: Andres Duany and Elizabeth Plater-Zyberk—p. 25.

Photos © Michael Mathers—pp. 50–51.

Photo © Peter Mauss—p. 115 (left).

Photos © Jason McConathy—pp. 98–99.

Photo © Michael C. McMillen—p. 5 (and p. 33).

Photos by Charles Miller, courtesy *Fine Homebuilding* magazine, © The Taunton Press, Inc.—pp. 120–121 and 158–161.

Photos by Charles Miller, courtesy *Fine Homebuilding* magazine, © The Taunton Press, Inc.; Architect: Ross Chapin, Wash.—pp. 118–119.

Photos by Charles Miller, courtesy *Fine Homebuilding* magazine, © The Taunton Press, Inc.; Builder: Robert Malone, Baywood Building & Design Co., Berkeley, Calif.—pp. 123–125.

Photo © Martin Miller/Positive Images—p. 20 (bottom).

Photo © Bret Morgan/Esto Photographics—p. 175 (top).

Photo © Michael Mueller—p. 3 (and p. 173).

Photo courtesy National Museum of American Art, Washington, D.C./Art Resource, N.Y.—p. 44.

Photos © Susan Oristaglio/Esto Photographics—pp. 23 and 30.

Photos © Randy O'Rourke—pp. 34 and 88–89.

Photos © Randy O'Rourke; Architects: Maria Aurelia and Charles Fick—pp. 130–131.